E.A Adeboye, *General Overseer*
The Redeemed Christian Church of God
Hearing & Knowing the Voice of GOD
J.E Bamidele Sturdivant

Hearing & Knowing the Voice of God

Paperback ISBN 978-0-9893873-1-6
eBook ISBN 978-0-9893873-2-3
Library of Congress Control Number 2013940023

Published by
GodKulture Publishing
Chicago, Illinois

Phone: 815 630 9890
Email: publishing@Godkulture.org
www.Godkulturepublishing.com

Printed in the United States of America

This book is dedicated to every *true man and woman* of God; who daily seeks the *face* of God, to get revelation on the *Word* of God, to convey its truth to the *people* of God. May the *mind* of God be revealed to you all! Amen.

For the time will come when they will not endure sound doctrine…
…and they will turn their ears away from the truth, and be turned aside to fables (II Timothy 4:3, 4).

Rosanna,

"Keep your ear close to His mouth!"

Psalm 138:8

Appreciation

I humbly wish to acknowledge…

Lucille S.D Sturdivant (My Mother): Your exemplary walk in the Word has given me direction from my youth. At nearly ninety-one years of age, eighty years since accepting Christ, her motto is, "… *and you know what? I'm not tired yet!*"

Daddy and Mummy G.O (My Father and Mother in the Lord): Your life is a testimony to the faithfulness of God, and His commitment to those who abide in His Word. Your humility, holiness and continued prayers for my family and I, are 'gifts' that are greater than any materialistic treasure. May your well or refreshment never run dry!

Pamela D. "Modupe" (My Wife): We have been in each other's life for nearly forty years, married for 35. You accepted me on a promise, when we were just teenagers, and believed in me and my vision. Together, we have watched the Almighty God *surprise* us and keep His Word. *The Best Is Yet To Come*!

Contents

Foreword

In "Hearing and Knowing the will of God," Pastor Sturdivant broaches an extremely important subject in the body of Christ. Every true child of God should be interested in hearing from the Father and receiving instruction on how to navigate the maze of life.

From time to time we will find ourselves standing at crossroads of life or the threshold of a breakthrough without knowing what to do next or where to turn. This work will illuminate understanding and enhance our sensitivity to God's word, His will and our destiny-impacting decisions. God speaks eloquently and you need to hear from Him. Please find time to be still in His presence and listen for His voice. He wants to talk to you. Not just now but for the rest of your life.

God bless you.

Pastor E.A. Adeboye

Prologue

As believers, we have the ability to hear the voice of God and have a close relationship with Him. However, some are missing out because they have not learned how to listen to Him with their spirit. The only way we'll be able to communicate with God is by using our spirit to *talk*, *listen*, *walk* and *see* Him, because God is Spirit. This calls for a growing relationship with Him. Not only have we been privileged to commune with Him at any time, His Word is also at our disposal, to meditate upon, so we can grow in the knowledge of Him. You can get His Word so deeply rooted in you, that when He instructs you to do something, you will sense a prompting by Him in your spirit. It will be so clear, until it will sound as if you heard an audible voice.

My sheep hear My voice, and I know them, and they follow Me (John 10:27).

Thus, knowing His voice (Word, will, way, presence) is imperative if you really want to have an intimate communion with Him. It is impossible to follow a "voice" that is foreign or unfamiliar to you. What causes many people not to know the voice of God (and hence, our purpose in life) or trust His will, is that we are not familiar with His 'sound,' movements, wants and ways!

This book reveals fundamental principles that will assist you in knowing His voice. It will also help you to *upgrade* your walk with Him so that you can live your life as He *wills*, and not by trial and error. There is a breakthrough prayer at the end of each chapter. This will *improve* your communication with Him. Please, endeavor to pray them with all of your being, as if your life depends on them. In all actuality; your life *does* depend on your prayers. You see; how far one goes in their life hinges on their willingness to *act* on the instructions they receive from Him.

It is my prayer that God will open your eyes to see the deep truths contained therein, open your ears to hear the inaudible and strengthen you, not only to take action, but also to finish strong. May God's blessing rest upon you and make you a precious vessel unto honor in Him. In Jesus' Mighty Name, Amen!

J.E Bamidele Sturdivant
District Heights, Maryland

Chapter 1

The Voice of Life

> *The voice of the Lord is over the waters; The God of glory thunders; The Lord is over many waters. [4]The voice of the Lord is powerful; the voice of the Lord is full of majesty* (Psalm 29:3, 4).

One of the primary ways that we hear God's voice is through our spirit. Before the fall, Adam and Eve delighted in hearing the voice of God in the Garden. Immediately after the fall, the same voice that brought joy and comfort, now brought them fear. They were capable of hearing God's voice directly without any restrictions. As man began to spread across the face of the earth, only a select few had the opportunity to hear God's voice directly.

The Hebrew word for 'voice' is *qol* which sometimes has been translated 'sound.' It is possible to hear it without necessarily hearing and understanding the *voice*. If it is a spiritual *sound*, only spiritual ears can hear although to the natural ear it might sound as if it is just a natural noise. When Jesus was baptized in the Jordan, there was a voice from God that declared Him as His beloved Son. Most likely, only John saw the vision and heard the voice of God.

According to the book of John, chapter 12, when a voice answered Jesus as He prayed, some people near Him heard it as a thunder while others heard 'something' and without understanding the sound, said that an angel had spoken.

When Jesus encountered Paul on the road to Damascus in a vision, he heard His voice and instruction but all those around him heard a voice (sound) but did not understand anything. All these were supernatural events that affected the surrounding people differently depending on their spiritual development in God.

SPIRITUAL PERCEPTION

> *But God has revealed them to us through His Spirit. For the Spirit searches all things, yes, the deep things of God.* 11 *For what man knows the things of a man except the spirit of the man which is in him? Even so no one knows the things of God except the Spirit of God*
> (I Corinthians 2:10, 11).

The Holy Spirit is always available to lead us. It is never a question as to whether He has 'spoken' but rather whether we can hear and understand Him. Jesus said that His sheep hear His voice and that the Holy Spirit came to lead and to guide us into all truth. However, sometimes we don't understand because, we are not tuned in to hear what is being communicated. For example, an experienced mother knows what a child's need is when he cries. The more experienced they are, the more they can differentiate between the whimper for comfort, the cry for nourishment, and the cry of pain and discomfort. An animal lover can differentiate the needs of an animal by its posture, sounds and eyes. Likewise, God the Father, Son, and Holy Spirit are constantly sending us little *leadings* of the Spirit that we must be attuned to every day.

The promptings, signals and leadings of the Spirit are not given in a human language. We might in the end hear it in human language, but they are given in a *Spirit to spirit* communication. For example, when God speaks to a group of people and tells them not to be afraid, some may not hear anything, but feel a strong sense of inner peace.

Some may sense the remembrance of an event in which they had taken great comfort and faith, while others will suddenly remember various Scriptures telling them not to be afraid.

The voice of comfort produces different interpretations because we all hear the same voice in our spirits but our soulish realm translates it into something we can understand. Understanding this principle of Spirit to spirit communication is important, for it is the key to developing our relationship with God. We all do not perceive in exactly the same way. No two people think exactly the same way. We all are unique individuals. Although we understand and acknowledge that there is absolute truth outside of ourselves, and principles to those truths, we all perceive it in our own unique way. For instance, two plus two equals four. However, a baker may see it as two kinds of cookies multiplied by two makes four kinds of cookies. Or an animal lover may see it as two cats plus two cats make four cats, and astronomer may see it as two stars plus two stars makes four stars. We all add our perception to what is being *received.*

TRANSFORMATION

> *But we all, with unveiled face, beholding as in a mirror the glory of the Lord, are being transformed into the same image from glory to glory, just as by the Spirit of the Lord* (II Corinthians 3:18).

We are only limited by our ability to stretch our perception. Studies have shown that human beings normally cannot hear sound vibrations higher than 20,000 vibrations a second, but dogs can. Our inner ear does not have the ability to perceive it. Perception and understanding are always a construct from the blocks of knowledge that we already have to build *new* knowledge.

As an illustration, try explaining what snow is to someone who has never seen snow. You would have to use things within the person's life and knowledge to construct new knowledge. You might use cold water to illustrate the coldness of snow or use sand to illustrate the brittleness of snow. Until you are either able to bring the actual snow in itself to the person or a picture of it, there are some limits to what you can communicate. Therefore, there are things that the person can only imagine but not experience. Such as, the sight of snow covered trees twinkling in the moonlight with snowcapped mountains behind them.

When God speaks to us, our spirits hear Him, but we are always limited by the extent of the blocks of knowledge within us to construct the sum of what He is trying to say. This is why the more we *grow*, the more we can grow; and the more we *experience*, the more we can experience. The more we *seek* after Him, the better we *know* Him. This is why we need to read the Bible. It contains the recorded experiences of other people whom God has met and spoken with. As we understand how and why God spoke to them, we will understand how and why God speaks to us.

YIELDING TO GOD

> *I beseech you therefore, brethren, by the mercies of God, that you present your bodies a living sacrifice, holy, acceptable to God, which is your reasonable service.* [2]*And do not be conformed to this world, but be transformed by the renewing of your mind, that you may prove what is that good and acceptable and perfect will of God* (Romans 12:1, 2).

Our soul limits how much we can know of God by limiting our ability to translate the receptions in our spirit to our conscious mind and understanding. For this reason, we need to renew the soulish realm *through* the mind of God's Word. Our soul consists of our mind, our will, our emotions, desires and intellect.

There are some things that the mind cannot grasp but the emotions can. There are some things that the emotions cannot grasp but the mind can. There are some things that are completely beyond the emotions and the mind. However, if we follow our will (and it is in the right path), our emotions and our minds, with exposure and time, will rise to the occasion and be able to feel and know.

We learn to count before we learn to multiply and we learn to multiply before we do calculus. We learn to make friends and we learn what friendship love is. We learn to love our families and we learn what family love is. We will experience companionship, joy, sorrow, laughter and tears through life and finally gain the capacity to enlarge ourselves in our ability to love and to care for others.

In every situation you find yourself, God's grace has already provided you an answer and a way through it. Every situation you come across is an opportunity to learn and grow. There are some areas in life where you have full freedom of choice and in some, where the choice has already been made for you by predecessors or circumstances. When you confront these, God is always there to show you the right path, if your heart is right.

Understand and learn to interpret every perception in your spirit-man, every impression in your heart, every shade of your dream life, every tug of your emotion and every flicker of thought. Within them is the translation of the spiritual voice of God raising your soul consciousness.

> *Be led by the Spirit and you shall indeed be sons and daughters of God* (Romans 8:14).

Someone once said, "A miss is as good as a mile." Therefore, don't miss what God is saying to you today and every day.

GIVING ATTENTION TO HIS WORD

As we become more intimate with God through meditating on His Word, we recognize His voice better. Thus, it is beneficial for us to continually give ourselves wholly to this Word of life so that it can cleanse from our lives, impediments distorting our communion with God. The Living Word (logos) needs to work *in* us first before the Spoken Word (rhema) can work *out from* us.

God's Word is described as a sword: one is a sword that works *in* us (Hebrews 4:12) and the other is a sword that works *through* us (Ephesians 6:17). What has the separation of soul and spirit to do with the hearing of God's voice? When the soul and spirit are not clearly distinguished, we will not be able to tell when a thought, impression, sensing, etc., is from the soul and when it is from the spirit.

God's voice will always arise from and be in line with our spirit. It is through the *logos* that our inner thoughts and intentions of the heart are first discerned. No one can hear His voice until they first understand all that is within them – their inner thoughts, intentions, desires, etc. Only when the inner peace of God is ruling our hearts and our minds are we able to clearly hear His voice (Philippians 4:7, 8).

Jesus told His disciples that His Word (logos) had made them clean (pure) (John 15:3). When our hearts are pure, we'll see God and hear Him with the eyes and ears of our spirit. A part of developing the ability to hear God also resides in the edification of the spirit man. The spirit man is built up when we pray in the spirit (tongues). When we do so, the spirit prays although the understanding might be unfruitful. Praying in tongues builds up the spirit man. For this reason, Paul said that he prayed in tongues more than all the Corinthians (I Corinthians 14).

Many people that are new to praying in tongues find that their mind goes all over the place when they pray. However, when they continue consistently despite that, there will come a time when the mind becomes quiet and they will experience an inner peace. It is when this inner peace is experientially imparted that the hearing of God's voice becomes a reality. Peace is a very important part of God's guidance system. The direction in which we walk is guided by the way of peace. (Luke 1:79). This peace is not natural but it is *supernatural.*

Knowing that He would no longer be with His disciples physically, Jesus especially speaks about peace, love and joy besides speaking about the coming of the Holy Spirit. One of the first component parts of the fruit of the Spirit being manifested in us is the evidence of love, peace and joy in the Holy Spirit (Romans 5:1-11).

Peace provides the quietness of our spirit by which we can hear God when He speaks. We should pray in the Spirit and meditate every day, until the peace of God transcends our hearts and our minds in Christ Jesus. After understanding the dynamics of peace, many will ask, "What is the voice of God or the spoken word of God like?" It can come like an inner thought or impression, or an inner sense of knowing. One of the works of the Holy Spirit is to bring to remembrance the things which Jesus has said.

The Holy Spirit brings to our minds the Word of God (John 14:26). This can be heard as a thought process or an inward impression or a knowing. It might feel so natural that one can easily ignore it. Hearing from God should be a natural spiritual process for we are a spirit, have a soul and live in a body.

The key to hearing God is not in the development of the more spectacular gifts of visions or signs and wonders, although this can come as the Spirit wills; rather the hearing of His voice involves our mind yielding to the mind of Christ. The key is in our ability to discern His voice within us.

When God speaks, faith comes. The spoken Word of God produces faith in our inner man. The inner conviction and assurance of faith grows as we gain confidence in the hearing of God's voice within us. Ultimately, all faith is, is the impartation through the Words of God to us. All we have to do is to keep on hearing and receiving the *voice of God through the spoken word.*

Faith is the natural spiritual result when we hear and receive His Word. The Living Word needs to become the spoken word for faith to be authored and finished within us. God is speaking all the time but we are not always hearing. Blessed are those who hear God for they will have His faith. Stay strong in the grace of our Lord Jesus Christ. We are the sheep of His pasture and we shall hear His voice.

Breakthrough Prayer

Scripture Focus: John 5:30

I can of Myself do nothing. As I hear, I judge; and My judgment is righteous, because I do not seek My own will but the will of the Father who sent Me.

(1) Father! Saturate my spirit with Your Word so that I can distinguish good from evil. In Jesus' Mighty Name, Amen!

(2) Father! I want to clearly hear Your voice, please sharpen my spiritual ears. In Jesus' Mighty Name, Amen!

(3) Father! Draw me nearer to You so as to understand more, the Spirit to spirit communication. In Jesus' Mighty Name, Amen!

(4) Father! It is my delight to know Your perfect will for my life. Help me to present my vessel to You as a living sacrifice. In Jesus' Mighty Name, Amen!

(5) Father! Create in me a thirst for Your Word, because it is through Your Word that my faith is increased. In Jesus' Mighty Name, Amen!

Chapter 2

Hindrances to Hearing God

Having established what the voice of God is, this chapter will shed more light on what hinders most believers from hearing and understanding the voice of God. Remember, He is always speaking. Prophet Elijah's encounter with the widow of Zarephath is used to illustrate this.

> *Then the word of the Lord came to him, saying, [9] "Arise, go to Zarephath, which belongs to Sidon, and dwell there. See, I have commanded a widow there to provide for you." [10] So he arose and went to Zarephath. And when he came to the gate of the city, indeed a widow was there gathering sticks. And he called to her and said, "Please bring me a little water in a cup, that I may drink." [11] And as she was going to get it, he called to her and said, "Please bring me a morsel of bread in your hand." [12] So she said, "As the Lord your God lives, I do not have bread, only a handful of flour in a bin, and a little oil in a jar; and see, I am gathering a couple of sticks that I may go in and prepare it for myself and my son, that we may eat it, and die"* (I Kings 17:8-12).

NATURAL REALITY

Isn't it good that God sent a man to interrupt a funeral that was going to take place? How does this apply to hearing the voice of God? Even though this is in the Old Testament, there are some principles that are applicable to us today. In verses 1-7 of I Kings, chapter 17, Elijah had earlier declared to King Ahab that there would be no rain except according to his word. Later God told him to go to the brook, where the ravens brought his breakfast and dinner. He was well taken care of there, but after a while the brook dried up. Here is the insight from the text, sometimes we become so accustomed with certain ways God deals with us that when He changes His approach, we don't change with Him.

God cannot be put in a box because He is a creative God. Although God is the same yesterday, today and forever, life and circumstances will keep changing so that we don't get too comfortable and trust in our own strength. God demands that we be willing to change when He moves in a new way. God always requires our surrender because there are always new dimensions to ascend to in Him.

Elijah had seen the power of God working. It is a miracle for the raven to bring him his food. You might not realize what sort of miracle it is, but how many of you have ever been fed by ravens. Ravens are the stingiest breed of birds in the world, yet God used them to perform a miracle. If it is difficult to believe God for great things, this scenario should change your perspective.

When the brook dried up, most people would have given up, not knowing that God was working behind the scene. God's methods are not static, but changes depending on what He wants. Our trust and hope should be in Him because, He cannot be stranded no matter how bleak the situation may be. When Elijah realized that the situation had changed, he held on to God and listened to His voice.

If you can hear God's voice all the time, you'll never panic. You may lose your fortune, but as long as you can hear His voice, fear will disappear from you because your focus is on Him. If we can only hear God in every situation we face, we will be in perfect peace. The most secure position in the whole world is to be in the secret place to hear God. Take time to commune with Him in prayer so that you can recognize His voice.

In verse 9 of I Kings 17, God said to Elijah, that He had commanded a widow to feed Him. However, when he got to her house, she did not have sufficient meal to take care of her family. I thought that when God said, "I have commanded her," she would have been fully prepared for the man of God. Instead she puts on a long face, all because she believed that God had not spoken to her and she had not heard anything.

She never knew that her deliverance was on the way through the man of God. In the same way, God is speaking to many people today. However, they are not hearing Him because their focus is the *natural reality*. If you don't hear Him, you may remain stuck in despair without coming out of it. Hearing from Him is a major step to your liberation.

Thank God Elijah heard Him! What would have happened if he didn't hear? He would have died with the family. If the church does not hear God, all we will end up having is a religion. His voice imparts life, and with that life we can worship Him in *spirit* and in *truth.* As we seek Him truthfully, it is imperative that we renew our mind so that we can see beyond our *natural reality*, know Him more and thus, recognize His voice.

SELF-CENTEREDNESS

> *And she said, "As the Lord your God lives,* ***I*** *have nothing baked, only a handful of meal in a jar and a little oil in a cruse; and now,* ***I*** *am gathering a couple of sticks, that* ***I*** *may go in and prepare it for* **myself** *and* **my** *son, that* ***we*** *may eat it, and die* (I Kings 17:12).

How many personal pronouns are listed in that verse? It speaks to one being focused on *self* and not their *source.* If you are self-centered, you can never hear from God. Some people think that they can please God and get what they want by being selfish and greedy or covetous. No way! God's blessings only come on you when you hear and obey.

She was so engrossed in her life, her son's life and her peculiar situation. *Self-centeredness* can destroy! Christians do not realize that to be born again is to be born out of self into Christ, where it's no longer you who live but Christ lives *in* you and *through* you. The Bible says in I Corinthians 13:5a (NIV), the God-kind of love *is not self-seeking.* This kind of love is demonstrated in the life of

Jesus, who was not concerned about Himself when He was on earth. All He cared for was our salvation even to the extent of laying down His life on the cross. He had the power to prevent that excruciating pain on the cross, but He was concerned about you and I. This divine love will require you pouring out self so as to see as God sees. God wants us to be conformed to the image of His Son, so that we can confidently say like Jesus...

> *I can of Myself do nothing. As I* ***hear****, I judge; and My judgment is righteous, because I do not seek My own will but the will of the Father who sent Me* (John 5:30).

The woman, whom the prophet visited lamented that she did not have bread, but was preparing the handful of flour and the little oil she had. She only saw what she had. She focused solely on the natural circumstances of her situation. Gazing only on what you see physically can hinder you from hearing from God. Even if you have heard from Him, you might have difficulty in acting on what you hear because of over analyzing *your* physical limitations.

When Jesus beckoned Peter to come and walk on the water, he was able to do so for a short time because he focused on the voice of Jesus telling him to come. When his eyes were turned on the waves he started sinking. Likewise, when our vision is based exclusively on what is at *our* disposal, we begin to panic. It is a fact that because we live in this world, we have natural circumstances to contend with as we strive to reign in this life with Christ Jesus. But it is imperative that we guard ourselves, not to be overly focused on *self*, so as to be on course in our earthly mission.

If you develop a lifestyle of always turning to God whenever you face a mountain of challenges, no matter how threatening they may be, they will become small. Your challenges may be as tiny as a mole hill but that mole hill, could look like Mount Everest if you depend too much on *self* and not God. Every mountain in your life is merely dust that can be blown away by the breath of God if you focus on Him. If you can keep your eyes on Jesus (The Word), then you can hear God's answer for you.

Take the case of Moses for example, when he faced the Red Sea. He cried unto God because he realized he could not overcome the problem with *his* strength. God asked him to make use of the staff in his hand. The salvation of the Israelites came because he was able to hear God's voice when he told Him to stretch forth his staff before the red sea.

We live in a dispensation of grace when we can come to God freely. Jesus is available to all who can believe Him. The Holy of Holies that was shut up to many is now opened. Everyone can come to the Father God in the name of Jesus to obtain mercy. Don't be *self-absorbed.* Depend on Him by listening to what He is telling you to do, because He is more than able.

FEAR

> *And Elijah said to her, "Do not* ***fear;*** *go and do as you have said, but make me a small cake from it first, and bring it to me; and afterward make some for yourself and your son.* [14]*For thus says the Lord God of Israel: 'The bin of flour shall not be used up, nor shall the jar of oil run dry, until the day the Lord sends rain on the earth.'"* [15]*So she went away and* ***did according to the word*** *of Elijah; and she and he and her household ate for many days*
> (I Kings 17:13-15).

Another problem with the widow was that, she had completely lost all hope. She did not believe that God would provide another meal for her and the family. The fragile hope that was burning bright, has now been doused by her willingness to die, when she saw no way out.

According to Hebrews 11:1, faith comes from substantiating your hope. That is, you have to hope for something in order to develop faith for it. If you don't have any hope there will be no faith. The woman in question did not even have any hope left, so there was no way to develop any faith. She and her child were only rescued by the mercies of God, when God sent His prophet to her.

In any situation, even if your faith is not that strong to conquer for you, if you maintain your hope level, by trusting God unreservedly, God will come through for you. These are the three hindrances that prevented her from hearing God. What is the solution to her predicament?

Look at the words that Elijah delivered to her from God. He told her not to be afraid, but that she should make a small cake for him first and afterwards make some for herself and her son.

By these words of the prophet, most people would say that Elijah was selfish. Here was a widow so poverty stricken and hopeless, and Elijah wanted to be taken care of first, by using her last meal. But the way God operates is different from how we operate. The woman was self-consumed. God had to make her overcome that, by serving someone else first. Some of the greatest miracles have taken place when people forgot about their problem and began to care for others.

When you start to sacrifice for others *in love*, you put yourself in a position to hear clearly from heaven and experience the power of God. A good example of this in the New Testament was Cornelius who feared God, gave alms generously to people, and prayed to God always (Acts 10). About the ninth hour of the day, he had a divine visitation from heaven, which led to the salvation of his entire household. This was a man who was not really praying for his family's redemption but because he was consumed with the need of others, God conferred generational blessings on him.

God will sometimes ask you to do things that don't naturally make sense. However, if you obey, you put yourself in a position to hear further instructions from Him, which will lead to your blessings. The woman acted on the words delivered to her by Elijah. She acted contrary to her natural reality. Faith is about doing (James 2:17-20). You are how you *act*, not just how you *believe.*

God has many ways to deal with every one of us, as many ways as we all have different fingers on our hands. Remember this, He is much more concerned for your whole life, not just for your immediate needs. Sometimes, God knows that you must receive your healing in a certain way so that your life can be transformed. But most people are just anxious about the instant gratification and results.

God demands that we act in faith based on what we hear from Him, to demonstrate our dependence *on* Him before we can receive *from* Him. There may be many times when God will prompt you to give your last dollar, in order to position you for greater blessings. Taking steps against your natural reality like the widow, or Peter walking on water, is not an easy thing to do. However, when you agree with the voice of God, you will be victorious.

Breakthrough Prayer

Scripture Focus: Proverbs 19:21

There are many plans in a man's heart, Nevertheless the Lord's counsel—that will stand.

(1) Father! Because You cannot be put in a box, give me the grace to be pliable in Your hand, so as not to be a castaway. In Jesus' Mighty Name, Amen!

(2) Father! You are the strength of my life. No matter how challenging the situation I am faced with may be, help me to trust and hope in You always. In Jesus' Mighty Name, Amen!

(3) Father! You said in Your Word that, whoever loses his life for Your sake will save it. Enable me to surrender my will to Yours at all times. In Jesus' Mighty Name, Amen!

(4) Father! Your kind of love *is not self-seeking.* It is my desire to love like You. Therefore, let Christ's love be shed abroad in my heart so that I can love graciously as You do. In Jesus' Mighty Name, Amen!

(5) Father! Faith without works is dead. Whenever it is necessary, push me to act on Your instructions, so as not to be slack behind Your schedule for me. In Jesus' Mighty Name, Amen!

Chapter 3

Discerning His Voice

Knowing God's voice is not just a privilege given to a select few. It is the right of every believer. Learning to recognize His voice is a matter of spending more time with Him. It does not necessarily come automatically. It is also important not to compare yourself with others who seem to be able to hear God easily. If you diligently seek Him, He will speak to you in His time and in His own way. Studying His Word and meditating on it, enhances your spiritual senses to hear His voice.

FOLLOWING HIM

> *To him the doorkeeper opens, and the sheep hear his voice; and he calls his own sheep by name and leads them out.* [4]*And when he brings out his own sheep, he goes before them; and the sheep follow him, for they know his voice.* [5]*Yet they will by no means follow a stranger, but will flee from him, for they do not know the voice of strangers* (John 10:3-5).

Most believers really do not want to follow what God dictates in and by His Word. What we must establish from the outset is that God's Word, His voice, His will, His presence and His way are all synonymous. Meaning, God *is* what He *says;* He is the same as His purpose and there is no difference between what He would tell you in your prayer time and what He would *prompt* you to read in your Bible!

You can get God's Word so deeply embedded in you to the point that when He tells you to do something, He will prompt that Word in you. It will be so clear until it will sound as if you heard an audible voice. Therefore, knowing His voice (Word, will, way, presence) is imperative if one really wants to have an intimate relationship with Him. But it is impossible to follow a "voice" that is foreign or unfamiliar to you.

There has to be some measure or level of confidence established between the interested parties before there can be any trust formed. In other words, if I want to have a relationship with someone, there has to be a degree of certain things that are understood before I am going to be comfortable with the person, no matter how wonderful he or she may be. When trust and confidence merge, there is a sense of "knowing" that enables interactive parties to not have to doubt the integrity of one another. What causes many of us not to *know* the voice of God (and hence, our purpose in life) or *trust* His will, is that we are not familiar with His 'sound,' movements, wants and ways!

INTIMACY

> *For I know the thoughts that I think toward you, says the LORD, thoughts of peace and not of evil, to give you a future and a hope* (Jeremiah 29:11).

If you don't now take time to be intimate with God to recognize His voice, it will be difficult to discover His purpose for you. One of the frustrating things that can happen to anyone, is when a new calendar year is coming in and you look back and realize that you have not accomplished anything new in the past year. Then the frustration of not being on track with God's plan puts you under pressure to accomplish something large in a small amount of time. Be careful when you start making destiny decisions emotionally just because time is slipping away. Never base your decision on time, but in light of eternity. Time will stop but eternity continues forever.

Lacking consistent communion with God (prayer life) will make it extremely difficult to trust what He says or believe that He really wants what's best for us. Whenever you are not communicating, you cease to trust in someone whom you were familiar with. Who you were formerly acquainted with, without continual communication, becomes a *stranger* to you.

> *Then you will call upon Me and go and pray to Me, and I will listen to you.* [13]*And you will seek Me and find Me, when you search for Me with all your heart* (Jeremiah 29:12, 13).

God has a great *plan* for us but He wants us to commune with Him regularly to know the details of His *thoughts* for us. God talks through His Word, this is why it is very important for Christians to read their Bible. We can only follow His path when we know His ways (Word), otherwise, we'll be strangers to Him.

So what God seeks, and we need to hunger for, is a type of unquestionable "call and response" between Himself and us. Meaning, based on the trust (faith) factor that has been built as a result of our constant, consistent prayer life, when He calls *to* us, without question we respond!

> *Therefore Eli said to Samuel, "Go, lie down; and it shall be, if He calls you, that you must say, 'Speak, LORD, for Your servant hears.'" So Samuel went and lay down in his place.* [10]*Now the LORD came and stood and called as at other times, "Samuel! Samuel!" And Samuel answered, "Speak, for Your servant hears"* (I Samuel 3:9, 10).

Hannah has been praying so seriously for a child for such a long time, until the priest, Eli, thought she was drunk. She was not conscious of what was happening around her because she was so engrossed in her prayer. When she conceived, she fulfilled her vow by giving the child back to God for His service. After her son was dedicated to the Lord, she left him in the house of God with the man of God, Eli, to prepare him for ministry.

Then, when the child, Samuel, was about eight years old, God started talking to Him. He did not recognize God's voice because he thought it was Eli calling him, since he was introduced to God through Eli. After coming to Eli several times for clarity on the voice He heard, it dawned on Eli that God needed the child's attention. Then he instructed him to say, "*Speak, LORD, for Your servant hears.*"

Eli was benevolent to acknowledge that maybe he hadn't been listening to God talking to him. However, Samuel's persistence caused Eli to respond appropriately. God started talking to him about the flaws of the house of Eli that raised him. So likewise, when we call *on* Him, without hesitation, He answers!

> *I cried out to God with my voice - To God with my voice;*
> *And He gave ear to me* (Psalm 77:1).

PRIMARY VOICES

There are three primary "voices" from which we take advice. They are the voice of God, the voice of the enemy and the voice of the flesh.

(1) The Voice of God: His voice is His will, way, presence and Word!

> *It is written, 'Man shall not live by bread alone, but by every word that proceeds from the mouth of God'* (Matthew 4:4).

God is always talking. He is *I Am that I Am.* However, you will hear Him based on where you are in your walk with Him and not where He is. For instance, have you ever heard a sermon on one day that does not seem to have any impact on you, then, when you are facing a challenge, that same message begins to make sense. The Word became real to you based on where you were. It is not that the Word is different but you now *hear* it differently.

(2) The Voice of the Enemy: Satan seeks to "imitate" the voice of God with subtle variations.

> *Now the serpent was more cunning than any beast of the field which the LORD God had made. And he said to the woman, Has God indeed said,* ***You*** *shall not eat of every tree of the garden? [2]And the woman said to the serpent, We may eat the fruit of the trees of the garden; [3]but of the fruit of the tree which is in the midst of the garden, God has said,* ***You*** *shall not eat it, nor shall you touch it, lest you die. [4]Then the serpent said to the woman,* ***You*** *will not surely die* (Genesis 3:1-4).

There are some people currently in your life, that are as crafty as satan. They are not overtly destructive, but their agenda does not have your best interest as a priority. The serpent came to the woman quoting what God had said with slight variations. Everyone who can quote God does not necessarily mean it for your good, even though they came from God. Satan came from God, quoted God but was anti-God. His mission is to *imitate*, *duplicate*, and *fabricate* to deceive believers.

> *For Satan himself transforms himself into an angel of light* (II Corinthians 11:14).

Every now and then, God will give you the opportunity to see how much you have learned from walking and talking with Him. Eve was not the one that was given the commandment, Adam was. Yet when the serpent started talking, even though Adam, who was given the commandment, did not say anything, Eve explained God's commandment to the serpent. Adam was passively present the whole time when Eve responded to the serpent.

The devil is not impressed with your walk with God. What intimidates him is when there is a confidence or a trust factor between you and God, so much so that you don't have to doubt His integrity no matter what. The serpent is always going to try to tell you that your time is gone and not encourage you to stand for God.

(3) The Voice of Our Own Flesh: Our flesh seeks what is most satisfying and least confrontational to our soulish realm (mind, will, emotions, desire and intellect).

> ..."*O My Father, if it is possible, let this cup pass from Me; nevertheless, not as I will, but as* ***You*** *will*" (Matthew 26:39).

So then, how do we establish the difference between the three primary voices, especially when they all come from *within* me? We '*hear*' whichever is the most dominant the easiest! The most dominant voice is the one we nurture (feed) the most. The analogy that God gives in His Word, so that we will know His way, is demonstrated in John 10:1-5.

> *Most assuredly, I say to you, he who does not enter the sheepfold by the door, but climbs up some other way, the same is a thief and a robber. [2]But he who enters by the door is the shepherd of the sheep. [3]To him the doorkeeper opens, and the sheep hear his voice; and he calls his own sheep by name and leads them out. [4]And when he brings out his own sheep, he goes before them; and the sheep follow him, for they know his voice. [5]Yet they will by no means follow a stranger, but will flee from him, for they do not know the voice of strangers.*

A. "*...the sheep hear his voice...*" (Verse 3)

Familiarity with the shepherd of *that* fold causes the sheep of *that* fold to *only* respond to Him. Jesus is not only the shepherd but the *door.* It does not mean that there are no other shepherds...*nor* other sheep. But the sheep that belong to THIS shepherd, when He speaks, only have an ear for *His* voice.

B. "*...He calls his own sheep by name...*" (Verse 3)

The shepherd knows which sheep are his by name! He knows the distinction between what he has purchased and what name He has attached to what He has purchased! He does not just call them by a general name, but He calls them by specific names because He knows them.

C. "*...He brings out his own sheep, he goes before them;*" (Verse 4)

The shepherd *comes* for the purpose of meeting the needs of His flock! The needs are *Direction* "…brings out…," *Inspection* "…His Own…," and *Protection* "…Goes before them…"

D. *"For they do not know the voice of strangers."* (Verse 5)

Their familiarity with *His* voice makes them oblivious to the voice of any other *shepherd.* Any other shepherd would be a foreigner to the sheep! The sheep '*reject*' the leadership of one who does not '*sound*' like what resonates in their trust factor.

Breakthrough Prayer

Scripture Focus: John 10:27

My sheep hear My voice, and I know them, and they follow Me.

(1) Father! Give me a greater hunger for Your Word and sensitivity to Your voice. In Jesus' Mighty Name, Amen!

(2) Father! Help me to reject EVERYTHING that is contrary to Your truth. In Jesus' Mighty Name, Amen!

(3) Father! Let me not make a single move without You leading me. In Jesus' Mighty Name, Amen!

(4) Father! Help me to grow in my communion with You, so as not to miss my steps in the journey of life. In Jesus' Mighty Name, Amen!

(5) Father! Like a Good Shepherd, supply all my needs. In Jesus' Mighty Name, Amen!

Chapter 4

Growing Spiritually

And when the disciples saw Him walking on the sea, they were troubled, saying, "It is a ghost!" And they cried out for fear. 27 *But immediately Jesus spoke to them, saying, "Be of good cheer! It is I; do not be afraid"* (Matthew 14:26, 27).

Why is it seemingly so difficult for those who profess salvation, and claim to commune with God on a frequent basis to, on the same breath, declare that they have difficulty knowing when or if God is talking to them? They struggle with knowing which voice, whether it is from God, the enemy, or their own flesh that they are taking directives from.

The reason for the obscurity in distinguishing the difference is because, many so called *believers* never go beyond the *saved* stage to seek and establish a concrete committed relationship with God! They can *hear* God *call* them *to* come to Him, but never move on to maturity! Being saved is the embryonic stage of our walk with God.

PAYING THE PRICE

If we do nothing to cultivate, nurture and graduate to the various levels of spirituality, you can be saved for many years, die and go to heaven, but never fulfill the purpose of your existence nor enjoy all that was predestined for you to obtain! What's worst… those who do *not* progress, stand in danger of going backwards (there is no neutrality!) and being beyond help! God wants us to be steadfast, immovable, always abounding in our relationship with and our service to Him.

> *Therefore, leaving the discussion of the elementary principles of Christ, let us go on to perfection, not laying again the foundation of repentance from dead works and of faith toward God.*[4]*For it is impossible for those who were once enlightened, and have tasted the heavenly gift, and have become partakers of the Holy Spirit,* [5]*and have tasted the good word of God and the powers of the age to come,* [6]*if they fall away, to renew them again to repentance, since they crucify again for themselves the Son of God, and put Him to an open shame* (Hebrews 6:1, 4-6).

It is death to keep talking about the things you have repented from. Some people with a religious spirit have enough Word in them to argue with others, but not enough to convict them to live like Christ. Such individuals have not *grown* to the place of making a commitment to Christ. You can pray for them, but it will take the working of the Holy Ghost to change them.

Every time we go against the Word that God has spoken to us by sermon or scriptures that we have read, we are putting Jesus back on the cross from His throne of glory as if He has not made any sacrifice. It is, therefore, imperative that we know God's voice (word, will, way, presence) so that we are not an embarrassment to the Body; we can discontinue making detrimental choices, and we can live the abundant life that is promised to us (John 10:10b), leaving a legacy to future generations!

> *Be diligent to present yourself approved to God, a worker who does not need to be ashamed, rightly dividing the word of truth* (II Timothy 2:15).

The problem with not purposing to establish this type of intimacy with God on a daily basis is that, when *choices*, *chaos* or *crisis* come in our lives, it is extremely hard to discern the direction God is leading. Why? Our soulish realm (mind, will, emotions, intellect, desires) flares up and we respond out of *feelings* (fears) as opposed to *faith*!

Wherever the *static* of the world is on the line, it makes it difficult to hear the *standard* of the Word trying to play across your frequency of faith!

Some people have God's Word in them, but as they move further away from where they know God, they start losing the ability to hear Him. It has nothing to do with the devil but the movement away from the Source!

SOME INTERRUPTIONS

> *Then He spoke many things to them in parables, saying: "Behold, a sower went out to sow.* [4]*And as he sowed, some seed fell by the* ***wayside****; and the birds came and devoured them.* [5]*Some fell on* ***stony places****, where they did not have much earth; and they immediately sprang up because they had no depth of earth.* [7]*And some fell among* ***thorns****, and the thorns sprang up and choked them.* [8]*But others fell on* ***good ground*** *and yielded a crop: some a hundredfold, some sixty, some thirty.* [19]*When anyone hears the word of the kingdom, and does not understand it, then the wicked one comes and snatches away what was sown in his heart. This is he who received seed by the* ***wayside.*** [20]*But he who received the seed on* ***stony places****, this is he who hears the word and immediately receives it with joy;* [21]*yet he has* ***no root*** *in himself, but endures only for a while. For when tribulation or persecution arises because of the word, immediately he stumbles.* [22]*Now he who received seed among the* ***thorns*** *is he who hears the word, and the cares of this world and the deceitfulness of riches choke the word, and he becomes unfruitful.* [23]*But he who received seed on the* ***good ground*** *is he who hears the word and understands it, who indeed bears fruit and produces: some a hundredfold, some sixty, some thirty"* (Matthew 13:3-5,7,8,19-23).

The Word is a seed that's been sown. These are the four (4) types of ground (hearts of the people) that receive the seed (Word). The problem is neither the sower nor the seed. However, everything has to do with the ground. The sower is the one who is bringing forth the Word; the seed is the Word itself, whereas the ground is the heart or the condition of the people taking in the Word.

There are four types of ground receiving the Word when it is sent forth. Three types of the ground do nothing with what is being received that will have a lasting effect on them. This illustrates, by ratio, that at every gathering, only one out of four people who hear a message actually acts on it and profits by it. Thus by interpretation, when you choose your friend(s), only one out of four that you pick may be good *for* you. But the struggle is, why do I always pick the three? I should not be mad at them because the Word already informed me that there are three. The challenge is that I do not know enough Word to not pick them. This eliminates me from *blaming* the three for being unproductive assets to my life.

The four types of ground are the hearts of those who hear:

Group 1: They *hear,* but they do not understand what they've heard! (Verse 4, 19; They Have No Revelation). As soon as they are challenged, the enemy can snatch it from them. They know the Word but they are not grounded enough to defeat the enemy. In the *preaching* of the Word one may get energized to do something. But in the *teaching,* not only are you energized, but you also get understanding. What is needed to get and *keep* the victory over the enemy is, not mere *emotionalism,* but also the *education* to know the voice of God when one hears it, and how to apply it.

Group 2: They have *no depth* to their spiritual walk! (Verse 5, 20, 21; They Have No Depth). This set of people receive the Word with joy, but it has no root in them. They endure only for a while, but when tribulation or persecution arises to test their confidence in the Word that they have received, they immediately stumble. The proof of whether you believe what you claim that you know, is in what you *do* when what you *thought* you believed comes under attack.

Group 3: They are *not stable* enough spiritually to handle prosperity! (Verse 7, 22; They Have No Stability). These individuals are a little better than the previous group. They have *some* root to them, but *the problems* or *levels of prosperity* causes them to turn their focus from the One who *is* their Source, and rely on their "resource."

Hearing and knowing God's voice puts the believer in the last category...

Group 4: These *understand* and are continuously productive! (Verse 8, 23; They Have Constant Elevation). Every believer who stands on and stays in the Word prospers with it. There are various levels of elevation according to this text. However, no believer should ever be (based on this scripture) below thirty fold in their productivity. In other words, God expects us to be profiting, regardless of the level we are in our faith walk.

So then, establishing a discerning ear for the voice of God, prior to a storm, makes it *easier* to know Him while in the midst of a storm! You won't have to wonder, "Is this God?" when life's challenges come. As a matter of fact, sometimes God is the One who is sending you into the storm that you are experiencing!

THE PURPOSE OF STORMS

> *...made His disciples get into the boat...in the middle of the sea, tossed by the waves...* (Matthew 14:22, 24).

Jesus sent His disciples into the storm *by* His Word, but not *with* His physical presence. He was *with* them because they were where *He* told them to be. They had to make it where He sent them, because His Word is with them. LISTEN, every storm is not a crisis. Sometimes, we can experience storms when we are right where the Master told us to be.

Here is one of the key reasons why many miss it when trying to hear God's voice. We simply misunderstand (no revelation) the ways of God! We think that God should direct us in a way that feels good to us. However, some truths we learn concerning God's will for us can only be realized in stormy situations. Storms have a way of separating those who are *pretenders* from those who are *genuine*. It serves as a barometer. What then, is the benefit of a storm in one's life as it relates to *Hearing and Knowing the Voice of God*, and distinguishing His voice from all others? The storm is necessary to:

(1) Expose How Well We Know Him!

> *... when the disciples saw Him... "It is a ghost!"...* (Matthew 14:26).

How can you walk with someone for so long, not know Him when you see Him coming, and call Him a *Ghost?*

The turbulence of their environment, coupled with the instability of their emotions, birthed a *fear* that made them not recognize deliverance! When you act out of your emotion because of the crisis you are in, even your breakthrough can terrify you. Some people are afraid to be delivered because they are comfortable with what they have become accustomed to while in a bondage situation. However, times of chaos around us expose how little we remember what the Lord has both said and done in past events. The emotion of the moment overrides the truth of His Word and Presence!

(2) Challenge You To Move From The Familiar By Faith!

> ...*when Peter had come down out of the boat...* (Matthew 14:29).

God's voice in the midst of a storm will cause you to leave folk who are just like you in the stormiest season of your life. It is for your own good that you leave those who are limited or unable to assist you. Don't just walk away, but do something that no one has ever done before. It is doable to achieve the impossible because, Jesus' presence is with you. You must take control of your circumstances, by His word, so that it does not cause you to be emotionally out of control. Some are content to stay with what is familiar... even at the risk of not progressing! Why? Because the fear of loneliness is greater than the forfeiture of one's destiny!

(3) Determine How Well We Handle Correction!

> *...when he saw that the wind was boisterous, he cried out..."Lord, save me!"...Jesus said unto him, O you of little faith, why did you doubt?* (Matthew 14:30, 31).

Jesus was disciplining and challenging Peter for not going farther than he did even though he started well. He began to sink when he started looking at his environment, thereby allowing his emotions to destabilize his faith. In the middle of the storm, the Lord grabbed him by the hand and started rebuking him when he started drowning. The Lord reprimanded him in the middle of what he was afraid to confront. Notice, while Jesus is correcting him, the storm has no effect *on* him because he was receiving fresh Word from the Bread of Life. If you ever learn to accept rebuke, you will be head and shoulders above other people who started out before you or that you have to walk away from.

If you are not spiritually progressing, you are retarded. Submitting to correction is a sign of maturity as well as *sonship* (Hebrews 12:5-8). To run when corrected or to shut down as many term it, is proof that there is no level of commitment (trust) to the One who is correcting you! Before you get angry at being corrected, look at Who is correcting you. The same One who *corrected* Peter was the only One who *believed* he could do it, *called* him out of what he was in, and *caught* him before he drowned!

Children need to understand that when parents are correcting them, it is not because they don't want them to *have* a life, but to *extend* the life that they have. Before you start to say, "*I've got my friends and do not need any family,*" it is important that you know that it is because you have a family that made it possible for you to have a friend. It is because of your good family orientation that made people want to associate with you. It is your family that will be with you and love you unconditionally when you are down. They are the ones that never change. You embrace the correction of God because you believe you are His. How well have you *learned* God's voice?

Breakthrough Prayer

Scripture Focus: Hebrews 6:1

Therefore, leaving the discussion of the elementary principles of Christ, let us go on to perfection, not laying again the foundation of repentance from dead works and of faith toward God.

(1) Father! Let me hear You *NOW* clearer than any other time in my life (I Samuel 3:1). In Jesus' Mighty Name, Amen!

(2) Father! Get rid of any 'static' that seeks to hinder me from hearing You (Isaiah 30:9). In Jesus' Mighty Name, Amen!

(3) Father! Remove the wax of worldly wisdom from my ears (Matthew 13:15). In Jesus' Mighty Name, Amen!

(4) Father! Give me a better knowledge of You by every storm that I go through (Psalm 119:67). In Jesus' Mighty Name, Amen!

(5) Father! Empower me to be rooted and grounded in love, so that I may be able to know the love of Christ which passes knowledge and also attain the fullness of God (Ephesians 3:16-19). In Jesus' Mighty Name, Amen!

Chapter 5

Embracing His Truth

All Scripture is given by inspiration of God, and is profitable for doctrine, for reproof, for correction, for instruction in righteousness, [17] *that the man of God may be complete, thoroughly equipped for every good work* (II Timothy 3:16, 17).

All scripture is not handed to us by our request, but it is given to us as a gift. Do you really understand what you have in your possession each time you hold a Bible in your hands or read its verses? Yes, it is the *Word* of God, but it is also the *will* of God! It's what He likes, dislikes, loves, hates, desires, thinks and feels. It contains *His* emotions. In the Bible, we find out what makes Him *cry, grieve, angry and regret.*

GOD'S EMOTIONS

(1) Cry: God cries when His people miss opportunities because they didn't recognize their *season.* This is because they don't take time out to discover it. It is a sad thing to now be struggling to make up for something that should have happened for you ten years ago.

> *Now as He drew near, He saw the city and wept over it, [42] saying, "If you had known, even you, especially in this your day, the things that make for your peace! But now they are hidden from your eyes. [43] For days will come upon you when your enemies will build an embankment around you, surround you and close you in on every side, [44] and level you, and your children within you, to the ground; and they will not leave in you one stone upon another, because you did not know the time of your visitation"* (Luke 19:41-44).

(2) Grieve: A work of the flesh grieves Him. We upset Him when our conduct does not line up with our Christian confession. Our lives have to line-up with our lips. It is very terrifying that some people in a high leadership position may not have anything to show for their work in this world because of their hypocritical life. Our daily prayer to God should be, "*Let every Word I speak and my lifestyle glorify* **You**," instead of praying to Him to give us various things that have no lasting value.

> *Let no corrupt word proceed out of your mouth, but what is good for necessary edification, that it may impart grace to the* hearers. [30]*And do not grieve the Holy Spirit of God, by whom you were sealed for the day of redemption* (Ephesians 4:29, 30).

(3) Angry: We annoy God when we fail to maintain *pure* commitment. With reference to the scripture below, God was so angry with this people, that He allowed them to fall into the hands of their enemies. They not only did wrong, but persisted in doing wrong! The more opportunities He gave them, the more idolatry they engaged in. That's what David did not want to happen to him and his people after he took a census of them. He rather preferred to be disciplined by God than to be given into the hands of his enemies or experience three years of famine (I Chronicles 21:12). Can you imagine what would happen to you when you are subjected to the hands of your foes?

> *Then the children of Israel **again** did evil in the sight of the LORD, and served the Baals and the Ashtoreths, the gods of Syria, the gods of Sidon,...; and they forsook the LORD and did not serve Him.* 7 *So the anger of the LORD was hot against Israel; and He sold them into the hands of the Philistines and into the hands of the people of Ammon* (Judges 10:6, 7).

(4) Regret: When we continue to live and think of *new* ways to sin, God regrets that He created us. The struggle we have with God is that the adversary has convinced many that God is *only* loving and kind. Much of the teaching that is out now, presents an *unbalanced* God that is one sided in His *feelings*. However, God is quite clear in His standards, unlike people who are emotionally driven. The Bible is God's way of letting *us* know what's on *His* mind! We need not ever be in the dark concerning how God is moving or thinking for He is consistent with His Word! He is neither fickle nor schizophrenic... He remains the same!

> *Then the LORD saw that the wickedness of man was great in the earth, and that every intent of the thoughts of his heart was only evil continually.* [6]*And the LORD was sorry that He had made man on the earth, and He was grieved in His heart.* [7]*So the LORD said, "I will destroy man whom I have created from the face of the earth, both man and beast,…"* (Genesis 6:5-7).

IMPERISHABLE WORD OF TRUTH

> *For I am the Lord, I do not change; therefore you are not consumed…* (Malachi 3:6).

It is a lack of knowledge *of* God's Word…a hunger *for* His Word…an adherence *to* the Word of God that causes so many 'believers' to get off course. As a result of the aforementioned, many go through life making fleshly emotional decisions in *reaction* to daily difficulties. If only they would allow the *mind* of God to direct them, they could have a *heavenly strategy* for their *earthly adversities.*

Just because we may be unaware of some issues, it does not mean that we are excused from the repercussions. It is our responsibility to read the Word so that we can know God more and be like Him in everything we do.

> *My people are destroyed for lack of knowledge…* (Hosea 4:6).

I remember talking to a brother who had a seemingly good plan to get married soon, but was surprised that I would not get on board with it. Sometimes, we have worked an idea out in our mind so thoroughly, until we wonder why God does not approve of it. God says *My* thoughts are not *your* thoughts nor *My* ways *your* ways (Isaiah 55:8). Many are making decisions without researching in the Word, and giving themselves to prayer and fasting before moving on with their plans.

No wonder there is such a struggle every time there is an attempt to study His Word, come to a teaching session or *stay alert* during a sermon. It's not a surprise that there is always an excuse, such as, "*something comes up*," or "*I am extremely tired*," or "*I had to work late*" whenever one purposes to be a Bible student. It is not by accident!!

The enemy (satan, the adversary, the devil, the tempter) knows that the *less* acquainted one is with the will, voice, Word and mind of God... the *easier* it will be for him to get *that* individual to *fall for*, believe or ingest the lies that he offers as substitutes for the Word of God. *Knowing* all the tactics of satan is not enough to make us fully prepared to stand against him. What we need is to know the Word and live by it so that we can know what to do when we are faced with various choices. One cannot be proficient on a job without having knowledge of its requirements or being adequately trained.

The necessary courses, classes or hours of study would be taken quite serious since the keeping of that job depended on them. Now, if someone will do that for a job that may or may not pay you what you are worth; bring in someone to replace you or fire you in a moment's notice - How much more time should be put into studying the *road map*

(The Bible) that will keep us while we are here and prepare us for the *hereafter!*

If you know the voice of God, in *any* situation, you can know whether it's God or not! It's not that the Lord moves in *mysterious ways*, as much as we are oblivious to the ways of God's movement! We are trying to discern *spiritual movement* with a *carnal mindset*!

There is hostility between God's way of thinking and our *carnal way of thinking.* Our worldly wisdom makes it impossible for us to receive assistance from above when we persist in violating God's principles.

Now we have received, not the spirit of the world, but the Spirit who is from God, that we might know the things that have been freely given to us by God. [13]*These things we also speak, not in words which man's wisdom teaches but which the Holy Spirit teaches, comparing spiritual things with spiritual* (I Corinthians 2:12, 13).

What Isaiah 55:10, 11(a) gives is an analogy concerning the Word (voice, will, presence, flow, way, emotion) of God, that will help in understanding the necessity of embracing His Word. We will lift four life truths concerning His Word here.

For as the rain comes down, and the snow from heaven, and do not return there, but water the earth, and make it bring forth and bud, that it may give seed to the sower and bread to the eater, [11]*So shall My word be that goes forth from My mouth;...* (Isaiah 55:10, 11).

(A) "*...as the rain comes down, and the snow from heaven...*"

(1) As rain and snow are sent to *purify* the air and *saturate* the earth to bring forth its potential (Genesis 2:5), God's Word purifies us and causes us to live an **"abundant"** life! We need God's Word as much as a flower needs rain, otherwise we could shrivel up and die. You will never live up to your potential without the Word of God.

The Word of God is a necessity in our lives because, when we are faced with storms, it is the Word that will strengthen us to both confront and rise above the challenge.

> *How can a young man cleanse his way? By taking heed according to* **Y***our word* (Psalm 119:9).

> *...life...more abundantly* (John 10:10).

(2) His Word comes from heaven above as a *gift*, given liberally without measure! The rain came from heaven, and since the rain symbolizes the Word, then the Word must be a gift.

> *Every good gift...is from above, and comes down....* (James 1:17).

(3) He keeps nothing from us! His vast wisdom is ours for the asking! In other words, all that heaven knows, He gives us freely without measure. Meaning, He is not stingy with His wisdom

> *If any of you lacks wisdom...God...who gives to all liberally...* (James 1:5).

(B) *"...and do not return there, but water the earth..."*

(1) God's Word, like the rain, has a purpose! He does not *send* His Word with an assignment without reason. In the passage below, there are two reasons why He sends His word. One is to *heal* and the other is to *deliver.* Yet, there are so many believers who live their lives in constant sickness and various forms of bondage. Why is this? As stated previously, a lack of knowledge of the Word of Truth and application *of* that truth, causes one to live as a *victim* of this world's system instead of living as a *citizen* of the Kingdom while on earth.

> *He sent His word and* ***healed*** *them, and* ***delivered*** *them from their destructions* (Psalm 107:20).

(2) God's Word has a destination that it *must* reach.

> *It shall not return to Me void, but it shall accomplish....* (Isaiah 55:11b).

(3) It is impossible for God's Word to perish...it must prosper! If we work the Word, we cannot go down. This Word is full of life and imparts life to everything we do as led by His Spirit. This is why we should always walk in the Spirit so that we don't fulfill the lust of the flesh.

> *...it shall prosper in the thing for which I sent it*
> (Isaiah 55:11c).

> *...My words will by no means pass away*
> (Matthew 24:35).

(C) *"...make it bring forth and bud..."*

(1) His Word stimulates, forces and provokes prosperity! ("...make it..."). In other words, even if the seed of the Word in you wants to lay dormant, it can't because God will make it do what it is supposed to do. It will no longer be hidden, but it will break forth out of whatever it is hidden in. The pressures it takes to get through won't kill its potential!

(2) His Word *pushes* the promise through the *stages* to assure its productivity! ("...bring forth and bud..."). Everything that is on that seed of the Word that is inside of you, may try to prevent that seed from fulfilling its purpose. But God is saying that His Word has to accomplish its mission. You keep the Word in you, not because you know how to pull it out, but so that when the occasion demands it, God will make what *is in* you to come forth *out of* you.

(3) Staying with the analogy, no matter what's on the seed...once the rain or the snow connects with it, it *cannot* resist harvesting! Likewise, if there is a plan, a purpose or a promise from God, in me, once His Word comes in contact with it, despite my circumstance, it has got to happen!

(D) "*...that it may give seed to the sower, and bread to the eater...*"

(1) What His Word touches *reproduces* after itself! It produces after its kind. The craziness of people in the time of recession is that they stop sowing. If you stop sowing, all you have is handful of seeds. *DO NOT EAT YOUR SEED*! If you eat your seed you may have a *meal,* but if you *plant* your seed, it will produce a harvest...which produces fruit...which contain *more* seeds.

> *...yields seed,...according to its kind, whose seed is in itself...* (Genesis 1:11).

(2) Every *entity* that is involved in the 'move' of the Word...benefits! God not only wants you to get back your *investment* (seed sown), but He also wants you to keep the process going. This methodology has future benefits and returns attached to it. Those who are stingy will never have a harvest, nor will they eat "the good of the land." God gives *bread* for the eating, but *seeds* for the sowing.

(3) Those who partake of His Word will not lack their *daily* necessities! There will be no need to look to tomorrow's concerns if we focus on His Word *today.*

> *...I have not seen the righteous forsaken, nor his descendants begging bread...* (Psalm 37:25).

> *...That it may give seed to the sower and bread to the eater,* (Isaiah 55:10).

Give us this day our daily bread (Matthew 6:11).

You can only make request *of* God to the same measure that you know His Word! He is not moved by emotion but by His Word. What have *you* been praying?

Breakthrough Prayer

Scripture Focus: II Timothy 3:16, 17

All Scripture is given by inspiration of God, and is profitable for doctrine, for reproof, for correction, for instruction in righteousness, 17 *that the man of God may be complete, thoroughly equipped for every good work.*

(1) Father! Let my hunger for Your Word be more than a passing craving. In Jesus' Mighty Name, Amen!

(2) Father! Increase my appetite, through circumstances, for more of You. In Jesus' Mighty Name, Amen!

(3) I decree that: The Word of God is my Companion. As such, I will study its truths, meditate on its principles and live the abundant life God promised me. In Jesus' Mighty Name, Amen!

(4) I declare that the Word spoken over my life *must* accomplish its God-ordained purpose. In Jesus' Mighty Name, Amen!

(5) I decree that: I will *not* die until every promise, prophecy and decree spoken for good, concerning me, has been fulfilled. In Jesus' Mighty Name, Amen!

Chapter 6

Aligning with the Truth

> *...I have come into the world, that I should bear witness to the truth.* ***Everyone who is of the truth hears My voice*** (John 18:37).

If you have difficulty hearing, knowing and discerning God's voice, it could be that you are living a lie. It is of a certainty that in the days of the Bible, the Almighty God spoke both audibly and directly to His servants, messages to be delivered to His people. However, when corruption and greed invaded the office of those referred to as "judge," people began to equate God with those who sat in the 'position' but did not operate in purity! Thus, they rejected *God* because of how His *spokesman* lived.

FREEDOM OF CHOICE

For instance, the sons of Samuel who were made judges over Israel by their father did not walk in his ways; they perverted justice for dishonest gain. Thus, the elders of

Israel complained to Samuel and asked him to provide them a king so that he could judge them like all nations. This displeased Samuel so he prayed to God. God told him that he should honor their decision (I Samuel 8).

God gave a warning of the outcome of their choice, yet He did not *override* their right to choose or their choice. He loves them enough to give them freedom of choice, *even when He knew it was not best for them*! If you know His voice, you won't make certain choices.

So as the people of God (the Israelites) 'moved' from a God rule (Theocracy) to a people rule (Democracy), the wisdom and counsel of God was sought less and less. It was only during dire straits or desperate situations that they remembered to call on the Lord! Sound familiar? God therefore, had His servants write down what He *said* (His voice) concerning matters and to refer to them whenever issues arose as He did through Moses.

Hence, God stopped talking to them directly. Instead, He gave them some laws because of their stubbornness. They were so keenly aware that the written words symbolized the very *Presence Of God* that they placed them in a *separate container* (the ark of the covenant: Exodus 25:10-22), a *separate facility* for it (the tabernacle of meeting: Exodus 26), and only the *separated persons* (the priest: Exodus 18:1-4), could *handle* it.

Only people who had been separated unto Him could handle it. As a matter of fact, if any one unauthorized even *touched* it, no matter how well meaning they may be, they were struck dead...*immediately*!

> *And when they came to Nachon's threshing floor, Uzzah put out his hand to the ark of God and took hold of it, for the oxen stumbled.* [7]*Then the anger of the LORD was aroused against Uzzah, and God struck him there for his error; and he died there by the ark of God* (II Samuel 6:6,7).

It is very clear from Uzzah's action and its consequence that we should not handle the things of God in our own ways. It demonstrates to us not only the power of the Word, but also the honor God bestows *upon* His Word. We ought to praise God for the ability to hold our Bible in our hands... *and live*!

This demonstrates why so many 'so called' believers have difficulty in hearing and knowing the voice of God. So it stands to reason that if we *are not* acquainted with His Word, we'll *never be familiar* with His voice, presence, will, etc! Our Bible, the Word of God, to many, has become nothing more than...

- A *keepsake* of family members' birth dates and deaths
- A faded 'g*ood luck charm'* in a cars window
- A cup holder on the desk or lamp stand(s) by the bed
- A d*o not enter* sign on the desk at work against *heathens*

REVERENCE FOR THE WORD

Many people take their Bible everywhere because it makes them appear spiritual. Yet, very few reverence it as *God's Presence* and give it the honor that it is due! No wonder we have such little regard for either the Bible or the God *of* the Bible.

When we fail to understand its significance, its directives or directions, then its creeds, standards and statues are *dismissed* as antiquated, outdated, irrelevant or unnecessary for everyday life! Yet *The Word*:

> *In the beginning was the Word, and the Word was with God, and the Word was God.* [2]*He was in the beginning with God.* [3]*All things were made through Him, and without Him nothing was made that was made.* [4]*In Him was life, and the life was the light of men.* [5]*And the light shines in the darkness, and the darkness did not comprehend it.* [14]*And the Word became flesh and dwelt among us, and we beheld His glory, the glory as of the only begotten of the Father, full of grace and truth* (John 1:1-5, 14).

From the very beginning, there is a lot of power contained in the Word. Jesus gives a *harsh* warning to those who trivialize the necessity of knowing God's voice, specifically through Him! In chapter 5 of the same gospel, Jesus says that if you can't hear His voice in His Word, then you can't hear the voice of the Father. This is why you cannot play with the Bible. It cannot be what you read once in a while as if it is a ceremonial book. It has to be viewed and revered as the *power* and the *presence* of God.

The more Word that you know, the more you are enabled to overcome what is not in the Word.

> *Do not think that I shall accuse you to the Father; there is one who accuses you - Moses, in whom you trust.* [46]*For if you believed Moses, you would believe Me; for he wrote about Me.* [47]*But if you do not believe his writings, how will you believe My words*?" (John 5:45-47).

If you can't believe God's Word, how can you believe He is speaking to you through it? There is a relationship between what God wrote through Moses and what God said. Thus, it is imperative that we hear and know His Word and His voice so that we can be sure we are on the right path. This is why Jesus said that the Holy Spirit will bring to our remembrance whatever He tells us in His Word (John 14:26).

If you read and meditate on the Word, it will direct your life. However, if you don't feed on it, you leave your life to chance. It is important to know the scripture for your peculiar situation. For instance, if you are broke, you cannot quote the scripture, "For God so loved the world that He gave His only begotten Son" (John 3:16) to get you out of poverty because it does not apply to your condition.

Knowing how to apply God's word to your life is necessary for gaining victory in any given situation. For instance, someone who is sick cannot declare that "my God shall supply all your need according to His riches in glory by Christ Jesus" (Philippians 4:19) because *that* scripture does not apply to *that* situation. It is wise for somebody in that dilemma to say, "He was wounded for our transgressions...and by His stripes we are healed" (*Isaiah 53:5*). You have to know what God says about your situation so that you are not ruled by feelings. **We must...**

COME INTO UNION WITH THE WORD

Now, in order for us to gain a more sensitive "ear" to the voice of God, there are various things that we can do to aid in that process (This *is* a partial list to get us started!).

(1) We Must Make a Demand on Our Leaders to Give Us God's Word!

> ...*They told Ezra the scribe to bring the Book of the Law*... (Nehemiah 8:1).

This is very important because some people come into church services after the scripture is read. God's Word is very vital. In fact, it should be the foundation of any preaching or teaching. No philosophy or ideology can take the place of the Word. God's Word is the standard and the final authority. Thus, one must refuse to accept a *watered down* version of truth that is comfortable and compromising, just so that they can remain in sin! God's Word will show us the way to live the abundant life which Jesus came to give to us.

I remember about five years ago when I went to visit my spiritual father in Africa. When I met him, I asked if he had a message from God for me. He replied that God was not saying anything because I had not carried out the last instruction He gave to me. This suffices to show that God does not care how much it may cost us or how far we have to go, He wants us to *do His Word.* Disobedience or partial obedience, for that matter, may cause us to *miss* what He promised or not receive what we prayed for.

(2) We Must Break Way From "Microwave" Messages!

> *...he read...from morning until midday...and the ears of all the people were attentive to the Book of the Law* (Nehemiah 8:3).

If the Word is not making you better, maybe you need to spend more time mediating on it so that it can transform your life. The Word is the most reliable *change agent.*

> *I charge you therefore before God and the Lord Jesus Christ, who will judge the living and the dead at His appearing and His kingdom: [2]Preach the word! Be ready in season and out of season. Convince, rebuke, exhort, with all longsuffering and teaching. [3]For the time will come when they will not endure sound doctrine, but according to their own desires, because they have itching ears, they will heap up for themselves teachers; [4]and they will turn their ears away from the truth, and be turned aside to fables* (II Timothy 4:1-4).

When God's Word does *not* restrain us from doing what we *feel,* we might be a tool in the hand of the enemy to execute *his* agenda. The *retraining* process makes many settle into mediocrity! Why? Because what has been insufficient has become their '*normal*!' However, if you take, for example, if all you have seen is what's in south east of the United States and you are taken to another location, the new environment becomes a new world. You have the option of either adapting to the new environment, which might take some time, or you can go back to your former place. In the same manner, when you are trying to embrace God's Word, it might seem hard because it goes against what has become your norm. However, if you take time to consistently meditate on it, you'll know what to do and say whenever you get a negative report.

(3) We Must Esteem The Word of God High, So That We 'Look Up' To It (Him)!

> *...stood on a platform of wood which they had made for the purpose...* (Nehemiah 8:4).

You must come to the point where you start asking God, s*how me.* One of the greatest books in the Bible that deals with God's Word and the power of it is Psalm 119. Every verse of it talks about the Word. It refers to it as the testimony, covenant, statutes, law and commandment. His Word is very potent because even if your circumstances do not line up with it, I have the assurance that "Forever, O Lord, Your Word is settled in heaven" (Psalm 119:89). If it is *so* in heaven, then it will surely be *settled* on earth. The devil does not flee from you just because you are able to fight, he only flees when you rightly apply the scriptures as Jesus did to defeat him in the wilderness (Luke 4:1-12).

> *I will worship toward Your holy temple, and praise Your name For Your loving kindness and Your truth; For You have magnified Your word above all Your name* (Psalm 138:2).

God magnified His Word above all His numerous names (Elohim, Jehovah Jireh, Jehovah Rapha…). It is of no use if you know all His names without knowing the Word that backs them. If you want Him to reveal Himself to you through one of His attributes, study and meditate on the Word that pertains to that. This is because wherever you "gaze" (focus) is the direction you will go in! *Raise* your *gaze* and there will be *elevation* in your *situation*!

(4) We Must Adjust our 'Posture' Based on His Presence!

> *…and when he opened it, all the people stood up* (Nehemiah 8:5).

Simply put, we must change *our* way of movement if we reverence *His* presence! Since He abides in the praises of His people (Psalm 22:3), then praise and worship should be our *priority*. If the Bible is His voice, then when it is being taught, we should be in attendance. It is only through His word that we will be able to *shift* in our ways.

> *I thought about my ways, and turned my feet to Your testimonies.* [60]*I made haste, and did not delay To keep Your commandments* (Psalm 119:59, 60).

Once we have been exposed to His truths, it is then a rebellious choice to continually *walk* in error! Many are tired when they are involved in spiritual things because they are so accustomed to carnal things. This should not be. Therefore, let us cast off the works of darkness, and put on the armor of light so as to overcome the vices of the devil.

(5) We Must Become Selfless When Having Opportunities To 'Receive' The Word (Presence) Of God!

> *...all the people answered, Amen... lifting up their hands...bowed their heads...worshiped the Lord with their faces to the ground* (Nehemiah 8:6).

Once the people heard the Word, it forced a new level of selfless worship to show how they revere the King of kings. God is trying to get more Word in you, to cause you to become more sensitive to His voice. For instance, on a particular day, you can decide not to say anything to anyone that cannot be supported with scriptures. This will drastically change your spiritual perspective, and cause you to begin to see as God sees.

> *And one cried to another and said: "Holy, holy, holy is the LORD of hosts; the whole earth is full of His glory!"* [4] *And the posts of the door were shaken by the voice of him who cried out, and the house was filled with smoke.* [5] *So I said: "Woe is me, for I am undone! Because I am a man of unclean lips, and I dwell in the midst of a people of unclean lips; for my eyes have seen the King, The LORD of hosts"* (Isaiah 6:3-5).

Whenever you are around certain types of people of like behavior, it is easy to become comfortable in that environment, because there is no higher standard to challenge you. Many respond to the Almighty God as if He *owes* them something when they are in *His* presence! We should respond with gratitude for Him allowing us to come in!

(6) We Must Be Open to Be Taught Both Intellectual and Applicable Truths!

> *...they gave the sense, and helped them to understand the reading* (Nehemiah 8:8).

One must not just *know* the truth, they must also know how to *apply* the truth! This is why it is very important to extensively give yourself to the Word of God. Then, no matter what situation arises, you will be able to handle it.

> *How can a young man cleanse his way? By taking heed according to Your word.* [10]*With my whole heart I have sought You; Oh, let me not wander from Your commandments*! [11]*Your word I have hidden in my heart, that I might not sin against You* (Psalm 119:9-11).

You don't want to water down the Word because you are guilty. In order not to give in to sin, you have to give yourself to the Word to build your spiritual immune system. Many have intellectual affirmation of God's Word but do not *allow* it to impact their lifestyle! The way to defeat the devil is to respond to him *with* God's Word because he only *respects* the Word.

In addition to defeating the devil with the Word, if you allow the *scripture to impact your life*, then *life won't impact you.* Ecclesiastes 1:9-10 states, "*that which has been is what will always be, and there is nothing new under the sun.*" You might think that what you are going through is uncommon, but it has happened before. If you don't equip yourself with the right scripture, learning from the examples of those who confronted and conquered life's challenges, then, you'll be defeated each time a storm arises.

(7) We Must Change Our Emotions, Attitudes And Mindsets Based On the Word We Are Taught!

> ...*all the people wept, when they heard the words of the Law...and rejoice greatly, because they understood the words that were declared to them* (Nehemiah 8:9, 12).

What we hear from the Word is not meant to make us sad, but to encourage us to know that we make God glad if we do them. Moreover, our lives are strengthened when His joy manifests through us. At first, we might not be comfortable with the Word when it convicts us. Nevertheless, as we persist in His presence, we will begin to rejoice at the noticeable change that takes place, as we change our mindset and attitude.

God's *truth* cancels out every mental, physical, financial, sexual and emotional *lie* that life, circumstances, past pains or the devil have told us! The choice is left to us!

Breakthrough Prayer

Scripture Focus: John 8:31, 32, 36

...If you abide in My word, you are My disciples indeed. 32*And you shall know the truth, and the truth shall make you free."*
36*Therefore if the Son makes you free, you shall be free indeed.*

(1) Father! By Your Word, let me see myself above every circumstance in my life. In Jesus' Mighty Name, Amen!

(2) Father! Help me to change my plan for my life based on Your truths. In Jesus' Mighty Name, Amen!

(3) Father! Convict me immediately if I begin to lose a desperate hunger for You. In Jesus' Mighty Name, Amen!

(4) Father! By Your Word, cancel every lie that life has told me, and that I have believed. In Jesus' Mighty Name, Amen!

(5) Father! Let my life be aligned to Your truths so that I can experience the abundant life You have in store for me. In Jesus' Mighty Name, Amen!

Chapter 7

Longing to Hear From Him

As the deer pants for the water brooks, ***so pants my soul for You, O God.*** [2]***My soul thirsts for God,*** *for the living God…* (Psalm 42:1, 2 (a)).

As a child, each year when school ended, my mother would send me to spend the summer with my grandparents in Virginia. One of the earliest memories of those times is of the deer that used to come and drink at the creak that flowed in the woods behind the house. Even though they were drinking to refresh themselves, they were also on the lookout trying to dodge the hunter's bullet. So it is for us as believers, while we are seeking God, we must be watchful, lest we fall victim to the enemy of our souls.

Be sober, be vigilant; because your adversary the devil walks about like a roaring lion, seeking whom he may devour (I Peter 5:8).

Have you ever wondered why some believers have a strong walk with God, while others seem to be stuck in the same place they were since being born again? I'm not making reference to pastors, evangelist or the like, but "everyday" ordinary christians.

What separated them from you and I? Why are 'they' able to tap into heaven's supply, get heaven's resources and hear from God, seemingly, so effortlessly and quickly while, for some of us, it 'appears' God turns a deaf ear to our plea? Has it ever crossed your mind why your walk with God has *not* progressed? Why you backslide so easily? Why you seemingly live so close to the "beginner's stage" of salvation? Do you constantly move by your 'feelings' and always have to have someone *else* pray for you? Is your quiet time bombarded with the static and the chatter of unresolved issues, past hurts, imposing problems, fears, loud laments and daily doubts?

COMMUNION WITH HIM

If you have answered "*yes*" to any or all of these questions, then more than likely your prayer life is in danger of becoming (if you still have one) an effort in futility instead of an experience to gain refreshment. Once you come out of a period of communion and communication with the One who is the "I AM" of all that there is (Exodus 3:14), being confused, empty, depleted, unfulfilled or deprived is an impossibility!

Job, as we know, went through quite a bit. However, when he came out of an experience with God, he said "Once I have spoken, but I will not answer; Yes, twice, but I will proceed no further" (Job 40:5).What he said in essence, was that when he heard from God, his perspective had changed. The problem with some of us is that we have not spoken with God, we have merely expressed from the fountain of our emotions, or the frustration of our circumstances.

It is impossible to talk with the One who is The Answer and still come out with questions. It is impossible to spend time with the Great Physician and still be sick, or be in the presence of the One who says, "*The earth is mine and all that is in it*," and still complain that you don't know how you are going to make it. As light and darkness cannot coexist, so also movement and stagnation cannot dwell together. If you have been talking with God, who is...

(1) Omniscient: All knowing of all that there is to know of all that makes up all that is known!

> *O Lord, You have searched me and known me. [2]You know my sitting down and my rising up; You understand my thought afar off. [3]You comprehend my path and my lying down, And are acquainted with all my ways. [4]For there is not a word on my tongue, But behold, O Lord, You know it altogether. [6]Such knowledge is too wonderful for me; it is high, I cannot attain it. [17]How precious also are Your thoughts to me, O God! How great is the sum of them! [18]If I should count them, they would be more in number than the sand; When I awake, I am still with You* (Psalm 139:1-4, 6, 17, 18).

How can we go through a situation with the God who knows us and then come out of it and not become better. This is why we have to know His voice. God already knows anything that we may ask or present to Him. No matter how deep your problem is, He knows the way out. This is the reason you have to be in constant communion with Him, or else you will run to people who will give you a *version* of what they think about you. Only God *knows* you! The challenge for most people is that they don't take time to draw close enough to God in order to inquire of Him.

(2) Omnipresent: With all that He is (He does not devoid Himself of His essence or power) He and He alone is in all places at the same time! He can be in Maryland, Texas and Florida at the same time. He is not limited by distance. He is the only One who is capable of answering prayers of so many people from different locations of the world at the same time. The devil has to employ his hosts to accomplish his mission, but God is everywhere. He sees everything. He is the One who gives us the assurance that He is *with us always* even to the end of the age.

> *Where can I go from* ***Your*** *Spirit? Or where can I flee from*
> ***Your*** *presence?* [8]*If I ascend into heaven,* ***You*** *are there; If I*
> *make my bed in hell, behold,* ***You*** *are there.* [9]*If I take the*
> *wings of the morning, and dwell in the uttermost parts of*
> *the sea,* [10]*Even there* ***Your*** *hand shall lead me, And* ***Your***
> *right hand shall hold me.* [11]*If I say, "Surely the darkness*
> *shall fall on me," Even the night shall be light about me;*
> [12]*Indeed, the darkness shall not hide from* ***You****, But the*
> *night shines as the day; The darkness and the light are both*

> *alike to You* (Psalm 139:7-12).

I remember when I was living in my mother's house, whenever I was upset with her, I ran up the stairs and locked the door, just to get away from her. It was still her house, her stairs and her door. The best I could do was to put my lock on her door but it does not remove the fact that I was still in her house. The same thing applies when we are angry at God. No matter what, He still owns the breath we complain with. He provides the work through which we earn our living. He owns the earth on which your house is built. Everything is in His hands, He is everywhere and we cannot escape Him.

(3) Omnipotent: This means that He is All powerful! Anything that *has* power only has the power that *He* gives it! He has ***no*** equal, nor competitor!

> *Who is like You, O LORD, among the gods? Who is like You, glorious in holiness, Fearful in praises, doing wonders?* (Exodus 15:11).

Satan is not the opposite of God and can never be equal to Him. *A created being can never be equal to, or know as much as the One who created it.* There is no other god like our God. Everything the devil tries to do is an imitation of God. Never give the devil the preeminence that you give to God. He cannot stop what God starts. At best, he can try to distract you to go off God's design for your life.

This reminds me of the song I learned in Nigeria, "When Jesus says yes, the devil can't say no." All he can do is bring opposition to you, to try and convince you that what you are believing God for will not come to pass. If you persist in your prayer as Daniel did for twenty-one days, even if it seems that heaven's response is being delayed, God will come through for you. Remember, He cannot be stopped! (Isaiah 43:11-13).

(4) Omnicompetent: This means that He is completely capable of doing what He declares. Some will say what they can do but then do the opposite, or nothing at all. When God says He will do, He will because He is the Word. You cannot deal with God the way you relate with people. You cannot give up on God the way you give up on people. God has a *time set* to bring to pass all that He has promised (Psalm 102:13). No one can "veto" what He has purposed to do!

He is *not* controlled, constrained or handicapped by the changes of life events! This is because He is the *I Am that I Am.* I Am is not controlled by what is going on because He was there before any events. This is the God you serve. The reason people panic when life throws curves at them is because they don't know His voice.

> *God is not a man, that He should lie, nor a son of man, that He should repent. Has He said, and will He not do? Or has He spoken, and will He not make it good?* [20]*Behold, I have received a command to bless; He has blessed, and I cannot reverse it* (Numbers 23:19, 20).

When God has His hands on you, the fact that people hate you or may not be able to stand you does not matter. Anyone who tries to touch you or go against what God is doing in your life will have themselves to blame. When God determines to accomplish a task, it cannot be overturned. If you can hold on to His promises, it will surely come to pass.

ROOTED IN HIM

> *Being confident of this very thing, that He who has begun a good work in you will complete it until the day of Jesus Christ* (Philippians 1:6).

What is happening *around* you never stops God, as long as you let Him keep working *in* you. Many get disturbed by what they see because they don't know that there is a greater work going on in them. In view of this, John the Beloved said "You are of God, little children, and have overcome them, because He who is in you is greater than he who is in the world" (1 John 4:4). You are not to be moved by what you see, or what you hear. Your confidence must be in the Word of God. You have to believe in what He says in his Word and stand on it, even if situations appear contrary. Based on this truth, the saints of old composed this hymn, "On Christ, the solid Rock, I stand; all other ground is sinking sand."

Some people are going into battles and some others are already in one but are losing miserably, not that they don't know how to fight, but because they don't know the right weapon of the Word to use.

"*The weapons of our warfare are not carnal*" (II Corinthians 10:4). You cannot win *spiritual* battles with *fleshy* weapons. It's like trying to fight the devil on his terms. So put on the whole armor of God so that you can be victorious at all times. Moreover, you are backed by the Lord of Hosts who has never lost a battle and who will never lose a battle.

When you are in communion with the God who is Omniscient, Omnipresent, Omnipotent and Omnicompetent, you cannot leave His presence confused. Spending time with Him will bring you to a point of clarity, resolution and determination! You ought to come out of His presence saying:

> *I can do all things through* ***Christ who strengthens me*** (Philippians 4:13).

You may be wondering, "How can I get my home when my credit is not good?" or, "How can I come out of depression and recover my joy?" You cannot continue to focus on the *negative report* and hope to find something positive in it. It is only Christ in you that enables you to accomplish all things you need to. *Some trust in horses, some in chariots but you will remember the name of the Lord, for His name is a strong tower, the righteous run to it and are safe* (Proverbs 18:10). All you need to do is trust Him unreservedly because, it is through Him that you can do all things.

COMMUNICATION UPGRADE

(1) Seeing Your True Self: So then, if you suffer from any of the following:

- I don't know what God is saying… Is He still speaking?
- Did I hear Him correctly, or if at all?"
- What does He really want me to do? Should I take matters into my own hands?

If you have asked any of these questions, you have to first determine if there is *any* un-confessed sin or secret bitterness that you have yet to release. This *will* block the "line" from God to you! This might be why your prayers are not answered, or why you are not hearing from God *clearly,* if at all.

> *If I regard **iniquity** in my heart, The Lord will not hear* (Psalm 66:18).

Iniquity is not just about sin, but also self-will. It is when you have to think that life is all about your self-pleasure. It distorts your communication with God. God might want to talk with you about some personal issues, but if you think everything is okay with you, then there is nothing God can do about it.

> *Behold, the LORD's hand is not shortened, that it cannot save; nor His ear heavy, that it cannot hear.* [2]*But your **iniquities** have separated you from your God; and your sins have hidden His face from you, so that He will not hear* (Isaiah 59:1, 2).

It is not that God cannot see or hear, but your self-will and sin have disconnected you from Him. Before you can start asking God for anything, it is imperative that you confess and forsake your sins, and then worship Him out of a pure heart. Once this is done, then He can reveal Himself and *yourself* to you. The more you *worship* Holiness, the more His Holiness *exposes* unholiness in you.

Isaiah received the confirmation of his call into the office of a prophet when he was in the holy presence of God, with *seraphims* (high-ranking angels) surrounding him crying, "Holy, holy, holy is the Lord of hosts; the whole earth is full of His glory!" Immediately the posts of the door were shaken by the voice of the angels and the house was filled with the glory of God. Then, Isaiah realized his real self and said:

> *Woe is me, for I am undone! Because I am a man of unclean lips, And I dwell in the midst of a people of unclean lips; For my eyes have seen the King, The Lord of hosts* (Isaiah 6:5).

The moment you see *Sovereignty* you see your *true self.* When you are in the presence of the Holy God, He forces you to look at *you!* In His presence you begin to see how inadequate you are and how you have used your tongue to speak guile. Some people might not agree with what you say God is telling you about them, but when they have a genuine encounter with the Holy God, they will see how wretched they are.

(2) Drawing Nearer to Him: Once repentance has taken place and the *disconnect* has been *reconnected*, then the problem may be, *not* that you do not pray, but then the *quality* of your prayer life needs to be *upgraded.* This is why David said to God, "*restore unto me the joy of salvation*" (Psalm 51:12). You shouldn't want to be merely *saved.* You ought to want to have endless joy in your salvation. Most people don't ask God to restore their joy because they don't want to be reminded of how they strayed from their progressive walk with Him. If you really want your joy restored, you have to look at what you did wrong so that you can make amends.

It is not enough to suppress what you are going through. If you don't address the issue, then the *suppression* can lead to *oppression*, which opens the door to *depression.* It is important to understand that some will always have a *low level walk* with God. But the question is "*do you want to upgrade*?" Some people are happy just to be going to church. However, it's not enough to go through some **"ritualistic routine of religious rhetoric."** ***God requires intimacy***!

> *Therefore submit to God. Resist the devil and he will flee from you.* [8] *Draw near to God and He will draw near to you. Cleanse your hands, you sinners; and purify your hearts, you double-minded* (James 4:7, 8).

Some of us want to submit to the devil and at the same time draw near to God. This is not possible because you cannot be moving forward and backward at the same time. **(3) Spending Ample Time in His Presence:** Many talk to God, but never *stay put* long enough to hear what His response is! It is not enough to just pray about any issue, it is imperative that we wait to hear what God is saying about it. If you don't stay put long enough for Him to respond, how do you know if He has answered your prayer or not? His response might *not* be what we are expecting.

Many times, we have made it seem like God's only response should be our will. Instead of saying *nevertheless not my will but Your will be done* (Matthew 26:39). We have reversed the order, "God not Your will but my will be done." Some seem to be making deals with God saying, "If Your will is done, then I will praise You and testify of Your goodness." Listen, God knows what is best for you. However, if you don't trust Him, you will never experience Him working out His perfect will *through* you.

> *I waited patiently for the LORD; and He inclined to me, and heard my cry…* (Psalm 40:1, 2).

Many cancel out everything they have been believing God for by being negative while they wait on Him. Eliminate all the negativity from your conversation so that all that you utter will be godly. Don't *talk* yourself to death. Proverbs 18:21 reminds us, "death and life are in the power of the tongue." Therefore, you are either going to *create* or *cremate* your world by the *words* that you speak. Since you will have whatever you say (Mark 11:23), you must not *say* what you don't want to *see* come to pass in your life! So, not only must you stop being negative, you must also eliminate negative people from your life.

If you do these things, you will begin to cultivate a habit of meditating on what God says you can do, be and have.

CONDITIONS FOR FRESHNESS

If these component parts are built up in you, your spiritual walk will take on a whole new dimension. Further, you'll experience freshness and a confidence that you have never known before! In my walk with God, I have always been a man of faith, but I have never been as confident as I am right now. I am very careful of what I say because as soon as I say it, it comes to pass. The more intimate you are with God, the more He tells you. To experience His freshness you must:

First: Have an *appropriate* time to talk with God!

Question 1: Have you established a time or place that you'll meet God every day? At a certain time, you have to be at the train station or bus stop so that you can get to work promptly. Where is the time and place for God who holds your life together? We have no time and place for God and yet, we claim we want to hear His voice. It should not be a Sunday affair. It should be our daily lifestyle. You have to know yourself well enough so that you can know the best time and place that will work for you.

> *O God, You are my God,* ***early*** *will I seek You…* (Psalm 63:1, 2).

(1) Commune with God *before* you get into the "busyness" of your day.

(2) **'EARLY'** implies making time with him is a priority!

(3) **'SEEK'** implies the 'relationship' is one that the writer may be passionate about and does not want to lose.

Secondly: Have a *commitment to tenure.*

Question 2: Are you willing to be consistent to *keep* the date that you establish with God? If you make a date with God, are you ready to keep your word? God will always keep His. How would you feel if someone made you a promise but did not keep it? It would cause you to deem them unreliable and unable to be trusted. In like manner, how do you imagine it makes God feel when you keep promising that you will spend time with Him in prayer and meditation on His Word, yet your life has shown that you don't keep your word?

> *...LORD, I have called daily upon You; I have stretched out my hands to You* (Psalm 88:9).

(1) Never think that you're strong enough to go a day without talking to or hearing from God!
(2) Incorporate worship with your prayer requests.
(3) Discipline yourself to continue what you start in *this* area!

Finally: Develop *pit-bull tenacity.*

Question 3: Will you 'trust' Him until the end? Many give up on God *too* soon! When Jacob wrestled with the angel to get a *turnaround* in his life, he said:

> "…***I will not let You go*** *unless You bless me*!" (Genesis 32:26).

You have to be resolute enough to tell God that the condition of allowing Him to go is for Him to bless you. You have to tell Him that if He wants you to stop praying to Him, He has to bless you. Sometimes, your best faith match with God takes place from *sundown* the previous *night* until *sunup* the following *morning*. Occasionally, you have to wrestle with God to show Him that you are really serious about what you are asking Him.

(1) Hold on to God during your 'darkest' seasons.

(2) Wrestle in prayer until your specific request is granted.

(3) Know *what* you're expecting, so you'll know when He's done it!

> …*Write the vision and make it plain…* (Habakkuk 2:2).

How are you sure He has not granted your request if you don't write it down? If you write the vision down you will be energized to run with it. Nothing from which we expect to obtain longevity takes place without effort or work being applied! It must be time tested and proven! You need to have a constant and consistent prayer life if you want to know His voice. You cannot know who you do not talk to.

Breakthrough Prayer

Scripture Focus: Proverbs 8:17

I love those who love me, and those who seek me diligently will find me.

(1) Father! Kill every appetite that I have that is not of You and make me hungry for You. In Jesus' Mighty Name, Amen!

(2) Father! Ignite my prayer life and enrich my fellowship with You, so that my life can be right with You. In Jesus' Mighty Name, Amen!

(3) Father! Trouble me in my sleep and throughout my day if I neglect to talk with You. In Jesus' Mighty Name, Amen!

(4) Father! Let *this* night begin *the* turning point I have needed in my walk with You. In Jesus' Mighty Name, Amen!

(5) Father! As I commune with You, *energize* me so that my walk with You can be *upgraded.* In Jesus' Mighty Name, Amen!

Chapter 8

Can You Hear Him Now?

Now go, write it before them on a tablet, And note it on a scroll, That it may be for time to come, Forever and ever: 9That this is a rebellious people, Lying children, Children who will not hear the law of the LORD (Isaiah 30:8-9).

We have already established that God's *voice, Word, presence, emotions, desire, will* and *ability* are synonymous! However, as we begin the transition from "*Knowing the voice of God*" to "*Recognizing when the devil speaks,*" we must seek to understand why there *is* a difficulty in differentiating between the two as well as the trouble that many have in discerning "*What their own flesh has to say.*"

THE RELIABLE GUIDE

The "sticky point," I believe (*and scripture backs me up*) rests in one characteristic trait or quality that is an *absolute* concerning the voice (Word) of God and separates it from when either the devil or one's flesh is speaking.

This attribute concerning the voice of God resonates unchanged despite a changing world or the changes we go through!

> *Heaven and earth will pass away, but My words will by no means pass away* (Matthew 24:35).

Meaning, this attribute is not altered by circumstances, economic changes, environmental shifts, political transitions, mood swings, financial upheavals or the like! If we are going to have any consistency in our life we cannot base it on emotions or finances. "Heaven and earth will pass away," but only God's Word will remain constant. This is why we should acknowledge God in all our ways and He (His Word) will direct our path (Proverbs 3:6).

What quality, attribute or trait am I referencing? ***Truth!*** You see, God's voice is going to absolutely always be confined to the area of truth! Clear, untainted, untarnished, *out in the open*, walked out…*truth*! One of the many reasons why we have difficulty in discerning our voice from that of God's is because we want to hear truth, but only in certain situations. Now, there is a disconnect because, we pick out *what* we want to hear and *when* we want to hear the truth. However, God *always* is both true and truth for, He is the same yesterday, today, and forever (Hebrews 13:8).

Another reason why we struggle in hearing if it is God's voice is because, we want to hear Him speak (truth) in situations and relationships that *we* have concocted that are shady, undercover, deceptive, manipulative, self-serving or deceitful! You cannot receive clear truth when you are operating from a platform that is founded on a lie! It does not matter that it's just *a little lie*; any mixture of error in the foundational *cement* of truth ruins the entire foundation!

> *You ran well. Who hindered you from obeying the truth?* [8]*This persuasion does not come from Him who calls you.* [9]*A little leaven leavens the whole lump* (Galatians 5:7-9).

It does not take a lot to get off course, it only takes subtle shifts from the truth. Hence, the devil is having victories over some believers because, God is not a priority to them. Consequently, if you are only moving from this self-concocted perspective, it will be virtually impossible to discern the *voice* of God. Hence, one will live a life that is fleshly or emotionally led. Further, they will be constantly disappointed when goals or objectives are not, seemingly, obtained!

When one does not have God's voice (will) directing his or her life, purpose (or the lack thereof) is then gained from environment, surroundings, trying to recover from pains or from looking at others. This is never going to accomplish all that one *could* have if God's dictates were followed!

> *The steps of a good man are ordered by the Lord, and He delights in his way* (Psalm 37:23).

To not move in the *light* of God's truth means that one is operating in the realm of darkness, whereas God speaks to enlighten! No wonder there is a *disconnect* between Him *sending* His Word and our ability to *receive* (hear, understand) the Word (voice) He speaks! When God sends His Word, you cannot understand it if you are operating from a platform of darkness.

> ...*God is light and in Him is no darkness at all.* [6]*If we say that we have fellowship with Him, and walk in darkness, we lie and do not practice the truth.* [7]*But if we walk in the light as He is in the light, we have fellowship with one another, and the blood of Jesus Christ His Son cleanses us from all sin* (I John 1:5-7).

There are no gray areas or shadows in God. Everything about Him is light. In light of this, David had the assurance that God was always with him despite passing through the valley of the shadow of death (Psalm 23). We believers in this present dispensation should have greater assurance of God's presence, because our covenant was established on better promises. So we cannot be shady and say we are walking in truth. The Bible teaches that when we stand before God, everything that we have ever done secretly or covertly will be revealed (Luke 12:2, NLT).

COMPLYING WITH HIM

So then we must conclude, that, the problem is not with the *voice* that is speaking, but with the sensitivity of the *ear* that is receiving! For you see, you can *adjust* your ear to hear what you want to hear! You can tune in or out, not only what you will accept or reject, but *also* who you will or will not receive it from and when you want to hear it!

Now, what has to be dealt with is the *frequency* knob of your desire, turned just enough to eliminate the static of lies that you have been listening to, so that you can clearly receive God's voice. He *only* speaks truth! God is trying to get you back on course so that you can hear Him like you are supposed to. If one continues to heed the deceptive *static* of this world's system, a lie will displace the truth of God in their life.

A few years ago, there was a report in the news, of a woman who was not pregnant but wanted to be pregnant so badly, until her body took on the symptoms of pregnancy. She was not pregnant, but she, through her strong desire to be so, *forced* her body to respond as if she was. Her belly grew and her monthly cycle ceased on the *strength* of her focus and aspiration. There was no child, of course, but it shows the power of ones thought life over their flesh (Proverbs 23:7). Likewise, you can be so focused on a particular sin; become accustomed to a particular lifestyle or habit, until you *convince* yourself that "*this* is what I am" or "I can't live without that."

God's Word teaches that if we believe (unwavering) concerning a particular thing, and continue to say it, we will have it (Mark 11:23). Listen, the *principle* stands firm, even if the thing that is desired is not positive! (**Get my book "Daily Confessions for Impacting Your World"*) God's principle of any two agreeing on earth as touching anything, be it positive or negative, will always be established. Whatever we bind on earth will be bound in heaven, and whatever we loose on earth will be loosed in heaven. This is why you have to stop saying negative things because the moment you utter them it becomes established when others agree with you.

> *For the* ***hearts*** *of this people have grown dull. Their* ***ears*** *are hard of hearing, and their* ***eyes*** *they have closed…* (Matthew 13:15).

Notice the stages that ultimately lead to the desensitizing of one's ears to **'receiving'** the voice of God. If any of you find it difficult to recognize God's voice, it might be that your…

(1) *…hearts…grown dull.*

Out of the abundance of the heart the mouth speaks. The Bible did not say that the heart has "*become dull*," but that it has "*grown dull.*" This implies that this is a process. This has taken place gradually, over a period of time. You were not always rebellious in your heart. It happens over a period of time ("grown"), when you lose a love for the Word or voice of God. Your love has grown cold. Your love for His Word or His voice does not happen overnight either, but it goes over a span of time.

> *Nevertheless I have this against you, that you have left your first love* (Revelation 2:4).

Do you know that you can be successful in a venture that God has not sanctioned for you? This will be traumatic for many well-meaning church folks when they get to heaven. Many will tell God that, "*I cast out devils in your name*," He'll respond to them, "*depart from me, I never knew you*" (Matthew 7:23). How can God say I never knew you? It is because they were not involved in what He called them to do. You can lose your connection with God and not even know that He is no longer there. Ask Samson! (Judges 16:20) Endeavor never to get to that point where you just go through the motions with no connection with Him.

(2) *...ears...hard of hearing...*

Your ears can be affected with what your heart feels. Whereas you used to receive readily and easily, now there are more *questions* before moving out of obedience. When you first came to Christ, your obedience was very prompt, because you wanted to please God no matter what. But now you have to critically analyze situations before you act. This was not the situation when you were begging God and making promises to Him so that you can be delivered out of a dire condition. As soon as He rescued you, you are now renegotiating with Him instead of acting on obedience.

> *And they commanded the people, saying, "When you see the ark of the covenant of the LORD your God, and the priests, the Levites, bearing it, then you shall set out from your place and go after it"* (Joshua 3:3).

The Ark of the Covenant given to Moses represents the presence of God. This is why it is abnormal to say that you don't follow God's Word (presence) because of the minister's lifestyle preaching the Word. When you see the Ark move, go after ***it***. That is, when the preachers stop following the *Word*, stop following *them.* You cannot use their lifestyle as an excuse because, God's Word does not change even if people do.

(3) ...*eyes...closed...*

Unfortunately, the Word or voice of God is not the focal point for direction any longer. Once the heart grows dull and the ears find it difficult to hear, then the Word of God no longer moves you. When do you plan to get serious about heaven? When is living by His statutes going to become your priority? You can deceive people and temporarily get away with it, but what can you do when you stand before the Lord who is altogether lovely and beautiful beyond description? He is the Righteous Judge.

> *You shall love the LORD your God with all your heart, with all your soul, and with all your strength.* [6]*And these words which I command you today shall be in your heart.* [7]*You shall teach them diligently to your children, and shall talk of them when you sit in your house, when you walk by the way, when you lie down, and when you rise up.* [8]*You shall bind them as a sign on your hand, and they shall be as frontlets between your eyes.* [9]*You shall write them on the doorposts of your house and on your gates* (Deuteronomy 6:5-9).

You have to love God with all of your being. For those who are parents, even if you are still dealing with one thing or the other in your walk with God, it is imperative that you tell your children what is right. Strive to *live* right because you only become right in the process.

Give attention to God's Words, incline your ear to them and do not let them depart from your eyes. Keep them all over your house and office so that they can be settled in your heart to direct your life. So because we don't think about God's Word that way, that's why it is easy for our eyes to be closed to the truth.

I remember when I went to get my eyes examined, my doctor asked me if I could see my eye floaters (small moving spots that appear in your field of vision that should not generally interfere with your sight). I said yes, but she replied, "That's not good because you should not be seeing those little things." She said that if I notice them while driving, I should pull over to the side of the road and call someone to drive me to the nearest clinic for immediate medical attention because, *the floaters should not take precedence over vision*! Similarly, it is a problem when the issues that should not surface at all are now your focal point. You need to pull over immediately and contact a true child of God to pray for you because, what should be the *passing* has now become the *permanent.*

REBELLION OR OBEDIENCE?

You know, when many face the truth they say, "I don't receive that!" This is so because they have already determined what they want to hear and who they want to hear it from. The fact that you don't want to hear truth does not make it any less true! Many have become so self-righteous and proud, until they have established their own "form of godliness." They go so far as to reject what does not condone their personal *appetites.*

However, as a good soldier of Jesus Christ, you cannot entangle yourself with such *superfluity of naughtiness*, because your desire is to please your Master (Jesus Christ).

> *Preach the word! Be ready in season and out of season. Convince, rebuke, exhort, with all longsuffering and teaching.* [3]*For the time will come when they will not endure sound doctrine, but according to their own desires, because they have itching ears, they will heap up for themselves teachers;* [4]*and they will turn their ears away from the truth, and be turned aside to fables* (II Timothy 4:2-4).

So then, if all of this is true, what is the reason that many have such a hard time with, not merely hearing or knowing the voice of God, but with *receiving* the voice that they may have heard or known? A partial listing of why is…

(A) They are not willing to allow God's truth to invade their areas of comfort!

> …*Convince, rebuke, exhort, with all longsuffering*…

This individual does not allow God's Word to come into some areas of their life, because it will make them uncomfortable. There are some issues that many do not even pray about because, they already know what God would tell them concerning it. It is important that you let your life be wide open to God so that He can give you clarity and direction in every area of your life. This is a *lengthy* process and many are too *set in their ways* to admit they are wrong. God does not look for excuses from us to justify why we live lies, He can only heal what you are willing to reveal!

CONSIDER: *You cannot be exhorted or encouraged if you will not be corrected!*

(B) Many have "numbed" themselves to the truth, thus eliminating God from talking to them!

...will not endure sound doctrine...

All that 'sounds good' is not necessarily sound! Having our flesh excited to *do* better does not mean we'll have the *discipline* to maintain what we start! Some things don't sound right because of the situations surrounding it. It might be okay in one area, but the conditions might not be right in the other. However, discipline is necessary to maintain the good walk you have started with God.

CONSIDER: *A "**wish**" can get you going, but a "**Word**" will keep you from falling!*

(C) Many can't hear God because they have already established in their heart (desires) what they want!

...according to their own desires...

Some cannot hear God because they have already decided that God's Word is an inconvenience to them. They are tired of *taking in* more Word because they don't want to change their ways. They really don't want to hear God, they merely want a validation or a confirmation to what they have already planned to do! Why should God keep sending you confirmation when you have yet to do what He told you to do?

CONSIDER: *God's voice does not come to* ***confirm us*** *but to* ***transform us***!

(D) Many expect God's voice to merely 'relieve' them of an irritation, whereas He may be causing the discomfort…for a greater purpose!

…because they have itching ears…heap up…teachers.

If one looks hard or long enough, they can find an individual (or church) that will say exactly what they want to hear! A lot of people, including believers, try to find somebody that will help to relieve them of their irritation without telling them that they have a rash. They go from person to person just to satisfy their itch. They continue in this, rather than (once and for all) confronting the irritation. They move from lover to lover, from drink to drink and from party to party just for temporary relief. They depend on people to *relieve* them rather than God to *deliver* them. God in His infinite mercies might be the cause of the irritation so that they can come to Him for help.

CONSIDER: *Just because the majority* ***says*** *it or* ***does*** *it doesn't make it right*!

(E) One cannot be turned away from the truth of God without being turned to someone else's "truth" (The Devil's Lie)!

...turn their ears away from the truth...turned aside...

You cannot fall *out of love* with God if you have not fallen *in love* with something else. That does not mean that you have jumped into it, but there is a gradual process to it. There is no neutral territory! One *never* leaves a thing or loses love for a thing without there being a replacement of that thing...somewhere!

CONSIDER: *Getting what you always* ***wanted*** *does not mean you got what was* ***meant*** *for you!*

For instance, after the Israelites pestered God to give them a king, He complied and gave them King Saul. Once God gave them that king, He *anointed* him to *make their life miserable.* Saul was anointed to do everything he did. Why? Because the children of Israel could not wait for God to select, groom and prepare David. This was a process that lasted over thirteen years. God has some wonderful things in store for you, and although you may feel that you are ready for what He has, He knows the proper time to release it, so that it does not destroy you. There is nothing greater than for a *prepared person* to come in contact with a *prepared place* at the *proper time.*

Breakthrough Prayer

Scripture Focus: Psalm 95:7-8

For He is our God, And we are the people of His pasture, And the sheep of His hand. Today, if you will hear His voice:
8 "Do not harden your hearts, as in the rebellion, As in the day of trial in the wilderness"

(1) Father! Let Your truths invade areas where I have become comfortable, so that my will aligns with Your ways. In Jesus' Mighty Name, Amen!

(2) Father! Give me an ear that is sensitive to your voice. In Jesus' Mighty Name, Amen!

(3) Father! Give me a heart that is desperately in love with You. In Jesus' Mighty Name, Amen!

(4) Father! Give me an eye that is focused only on you. In Jesus' Mighty Name, Amen!

(5) Father! Help me to obey You immediately and completely at all times! In Jesus' Mighty Name, Amen!

Epilogue: Obeying His Voice

Of all that is mentioned in the Bible, *Obeying the Voice of God* should be at the very top in order of priority. All through His Word the importance of obeying His voice and the consequence of disobeying it are mentioned several times. All of Christianity hinges on this truth. It is about a daily living relationship with God, through Jesus Christ, in the power of the Holy Spirit. The message of hearing and obeying His voice did not only come to Abraham, Moses and the prophets, it continued on right through to the New Testament, up to this very day. Let's explore some of the cases a little more.

RECIPE FOR GREATNESS

> *In your seed all the nations of the earth shall be blessed, because you have obeyed My voice* (Genesis 22:18).

The blessings of God came upon Abraham because of His faithfulness and obedience to what God instructed him. Thus, not only was he blessed, his descendants were blessed as well. The blessings of God can be imparted to others through our obedience and good example. Isaac became a beneficiary of Abraham's obedience, which is further passed on to his generations.

What about Moses? He had lived in the wilderness for forty years. Then, he experienced the voice of God through a burning bush that changed his life forever, and also the lives of the Israelites who had been bound up as slaves in Egypt (Exodus 3). From that moment on, God began pouring out His heart to Moses. In fact, God's voice was silent, in the Book of Exodus, until God encountered Moses. Once God had Moses' focused attention on His sign (the burning bush), Moses could hear the voice of God in a clear way. He received clear revelation of who God is, of what God knew about His people and how He was calling Moses to go and deliver them.

The rest of the Book of Exodus is all about a conversation between God and Moses, and Moses and God. Life changes for the better for us when we hear the voice of God with a commitment to doing whatever He asks us. In Exodus chapter 15, when God gave Moses a promise of divine health for His people, the condition was that, they must diligently obey His voice and do what is right in His sight.

Prophet Samuel is a wonderful example of the importance of God's voice in our lives. When still a young child in the temple, he heard the voice of God calling him. However, he thought it was the voice of Eli, his mentor. The moment he knew the voice of God in a personal way, something broke in the spirit realm that caused the heavens to be opened, and the Word of the Lord came afresh to all Israel through the young man who now could hear and recognize the voice of God (I Samuel 3). Samuel's life and ministry became a powerful force to be reckoned with as he lived in obedience to that voice. The testimony the people had of him was:

> *... Look now, there is in this city a man of God, and he is an honorable man; all that he says surely comes to pass. So let us go there; perhaps he can show us the way that we should go* (I Samuel 9:6).

You have to know God's voice to have a testimony like that!

What can we learn from the life of Saul? First, the same principle applies to a king as it does to an ordinary kingdom dweller. The key to life and leadership for a Christian is in obeying the voice of God. There is no substitute for that. Yet, again and again, we see believers trying to fulfill their obligations to God by every other means than learning to hear His voice. Disobedience cost Saul the establishment of his kingdom, and it can cost anyone the fulfillment of God's promises to them.

Saul was partially obedient. He did do some of what the Lord asked him but there was not a total commitment. His excuse was that he feared the people more than God (I Samuel 15:24). When the fear of the people comes before the fear of God, we can guarantee that we are going to lose out on God's best for us. There is no way that we can be obedient to God and at the same time, be living to please others. When we live to please God we will find much favor, but God has to come first, not the people. Saul had it the wrong way around. His fear of the people prevented him from pleasing God to the full. Therefore, God rejected him by overthrowing his kingdom. Disobedience to the voice of God is very costly. Please beware!

Three times in the Book of Acts we are given a good description of the conversion of Saul of Tarsus, who became the great Apostle Paul. The fact that it is repeated thrice gives emphasis to the principles that occur when we meet Jesus (Acts 9, 22 and 26). It has everything to do with the hearing and knowing of His voice. Even though Saul was a religious man, he did not recognize the voice of Jesus. It was not until Jesus revealed Himself through His voice, on the road to Damascus, that Saul was able to respond.

From the moment he recognized His voice, his will was given over to Him. The Lord used several different ways to reveal Himself to Saul. There was a sovereign impact, the personal voice to him, as well as the prophetic word that came through a disciple called Ananias (Acts 9). Those coming to Jesus Christ today must take a cue from Paul's encounter. We must have that "personal meeting with Him," where we hear His voice and know that we are now dealing with the Living Son of the Living God who talks to us today. Paul was totally sold out to what the Lord said to him at his conversion, even to the point of death.

BENEFITS OF OBEDIENCE

The call of God to Abraham to sacrifice Isaac, the call of Moses to lead the children of Israel out of Egyptian bondage and the call of Joshua and the children of Israel to march around Jericho to experience victory over the enemy. What do all of these have in common? In each situation there was the call of God to a person or people to do something beyond human capability! It was a call to obey the voice of God. *If obeyed,* there were blessings to be enjoyed. If *disobeyed,* there were consequences to be experienced.

Abraham, Moses, and the like obeyed God. As a result, God made it His business to bless them. What about today? The wonderful truth of the nature of God is that He cannot change, and He never will change. Where there is a person or a people that will listen to Him and obey Him, He bestows His blessings on them. As a matter of fact, in Deuteronomy 28, Moses declared to the people of God, what they can expect, if they obey Him. What held true then, still holds true now. Let's look at some of the benefits.

(1) Presence: When God talked about blessing His people, He gave them two conditions that were necessary for His divine blessings. First, they were to listen to His voice. Listening to His voice meant more than agreeing that He had said something, but it involved a willingness to go in the direction that He says. Second, they were to observe and do what He commanded. Often times when we hear the word 'command,' we immediately stop at that point because of our preconceived mindset of the word. The commands of God come from a God who loves us unconditionally, and always wants the very best for us.

It pleases God whenever we follow His voice or commandments. Thus, His presence will be with us everywhere that we go (Psalm 139). With His presence, we are assured of our victory every place His presence guides us (Exodus 33:12-23). There is a sense of inner joy, knowing that we are involved in what we were designed to do, and that is, to bring pleasure to Him.

(2) Promotion: The God that saved us and redeemed us has His own personal plan for promotion, if we are obedient to His command. We are shown in scriptures, individuals who were blessed as a result of their obedience. Why does God promote people who obey Him? Because it reveals that God places a premium on the life of obedience. Why did Abraham, Moses, Samuel and Paul excel? Because they placed a premium on obeying the Living God. God declares in His Word to the nation of Israel and to the life of anyone who will obey Him that, "*He will set you high above all nations of the earth*" (Deuteronomy 28:1). The word **set** literally means *assign*, meaning that God will assign a person of obedience a *high place,* because they cherish obedience.

The life of Abraham reveals what happens when a man is willing to obey God at all costs. In the end, God promoted Abraham. God blessed Abraham with abundant children and with real estate. How about Joseph? Even though he was sold as a slave and falsely accused by His master's wife, he obeyed God and left all the consequences to Him. Thereafter, God promoted him, bringing him to a point of being an instrument for saving many lives. He attained that status because of his willingness to obey God in the dark times of his life.

(3) Prosperity: When a person is willing to obey God's voice and His Word, God bestows His blessings upon that life, because there was a deliberate intent to obey Him. God declares in Deuteronomy 28:2, "*And all these blessings shall come upon you and overtake you.*"

God made it clear to Israel that He would purposely shower their land with ample blessings if they would obey and follow His commands. Any believer that will choose to obey God's voice and His Word will also find themselves backed by His blessings.

This book talks greatly about different stages of hearing and knowing God's voice (Word, will, way, presence). It is one thing to hear and know His voice, but it's another thing to act on what is being said. Hence, the onus is on you to obey His voice, so that His blessings can come upon you. When you begin to obey Him in little things, He'll begin to reveal to you what "*Eye has not seen, nor ear heard, nor have entered into the heart of man*" (I Corinthians 2:9). This is how you can influence your generation and generations yet unborn for Jesus Christ.

Will you make a commitment to God today? The world is waiting for the manifestation of the children of God. Will you be a part of them?

The Wisest Decision

Hearing & Knowing the Voice of God demands that you begin a productive relationship with Him. You must surrender your life to the Lordship of Jesus Christ. If you have not accepted Jesus Christ as your Lord and Savior, I encourage you to pray the following prayer aloud in order to receive your salvation:

Heavenly Father, I come to you as a sinner through Your Son, Jesus Christ who died and rose on the third day and is now seated at Your right hand. I confess all my sins and I invite Jesus into my life as my Lord and Savior. Thank You Jesus, that my sins are forgiven. Holy Spirit, I invite you to partner with me in my walk with Jesus. In Jesus name I pray. Amen!

This is the wisest decision you have ever made. Please, do not look back! Find a Bible-believing church where the unadulterated Word of God is being preached and begin to worship there regularly. Buy a Bible and study it daily.

Always ask the Holy Spirit to teach you His Word before you study. Welcome to the Kingdom of Light. May the Lord God bless and uphold you In Jesus' Mighty Name, Amen! I am waiting to hear from you. You can contact me through my address towards the end of this book, or by way of my website.

About The Author

J.E Bamidele Sturdivant, Sr. is the pastor of Faith United Ministries and is known worldwide as a blessing to the body of Christ. His unique style of simply, yet powerfully conveying Biblical principles has drawn millions to the cross and set the stage for massive deliverances and healings in the lives of God's people.

A native Washingtonian, J.E Sturdivant has made a divine connection to Nigeria through his God-appointed relationship with his Father in the Lord, E.A Adeboye. Heralded by Newsweek as one of the 50 Most Powerful world leaders, Adeboye has fully received J.E Sturdivant as a special son and poured mightily into his life in immeasurable ways. Adeboye, with the care of a father, named J.E Sturdivant "Bamidele," which is translated to mean *follow me home.*

Their relationship mirrors that of the prophet Elijah and his protégé, Elisha. As with these Biblical men of God, Bamidele has seen the ascension of Adeboye to greater heights in the Lord. In turn, the same mantle has fallen on him. Since their divine connection, Bamidele's ministry has been marked by the miraculous. Countless testimonies of actual resurrections from the dead, healing from cancer and astounding breakthroughs on every level speak to the authenticity of God's hand on his life and ministry.

A master teacher, Bamidele diligently studies to show himself worthy unto God and in the process earned degrees in Ministry. In turn, the sound Biblical truths he shares undoubtedly remind the world that holiness and excellence are the true hallmark of every Christ-follower. An accomplished author, Bamidele has written *No Longer Crippled...From Trauma To Triumph*!, which outlines the blueprint for a wholistically, successful life. He also authored sections of *From One Brother To Another*, an inspirational devotional for men of all ethnicities, ages, and social backgrounds.

His most recent releases, *A Divine Hunger*, is a forty day devotional guide which challenges every believer to live a life of holiness supported by an appetite for the Master's Presence. *Learning To Soar* is a step-by-step manual that goes to the root of one's adversities and teaches them how to rise above them victoriously. While *Daily Confessions For Impacting Your World*, is a forty day confession tool which outlines that meditating on the truth of God's Word and speaking it, works together with our faith to bring victory every time.

He was selected as the Guest Chaplain to offer prayer in the United States Senate in the presence of President Barack Obama, who was serving as United States Senator from Illinois at the time. His anointed and dynamic preaching style has also garnered the attention of other political officials.

He is a greatly esteemed and sought after teacher and evangelist who frequently ministers extensively throughout North America, the Caribbean, Africa, Asia, and Europe. J.E. Bamidele and his wife, Pamela D. have been married for over 34 years, and are the proud parents of four adult children.

Contact Information

For more information, feel free to contact J.E Bamidele Sturdivant using the mediums listed below. Although he cannot respond personally to all correspondences he would love to get your feedback.

J.E.S. Ministries
7905 Fernham Lane
District Heights
Maryland 20747
USA

Phone: 301-736-2383
Email: pastor@jesturdivantministries.org
Website: www.jesturdivantministries.org

Twitter: twitter.com/jesturdivant
Facebook: facebook.com/james.e.sturdivant

You can order additional copies of this book @

www.daforge.com
www.amazon.com
www.barnesandnoble.com

Also By J.E Bamidele Sturdivant

No Longer Crippled

Adversity. It's one of the guarantees that come with being human. We experience it. We expect it. But it's how we choose to deal with it that shapes our lives, both negatively and positively. Adversity can leave us crippled in our emotions, our relationships, and our finances. However, God, in all His grace, equips us with the prescription and therapy to heal us in those hurting areas. In this book, J.E Sturdivant shows us that with God working and moving in our lives, we can triumph and use adversity to our advantage.

A Divine Hunger

A Divine Hunger is a piece that will challenge you to grow in your walk with God. It is full of revelation knowledge from God's word on how to develop a hunger and a heart for the word, keep your mind on the word, live by the word and be liberated by the word. Many run helter skelter looking for solutions to their personal problems but the most enduring way to be secured in life is to develop an intimate relationship with God through His word.

Our lives glorify God when we bear fruit as we abide in Him and His words remain in us. This is only possible when we unreservedly commit to Him and value the relationship with Him above anything else in the world. No matter how gloomy your circumstances may be, this book will energize you and help you to experience the abundant life in all your endeavors. Be blessed as you read.

Learning To Soar

God's desire for us is to rise from glory to glory. As such, He has made provision for us to attain the greatest heights in life. However, negligence and slothfulness can open the door for demonic activity that brings about hindrances in our lives. These events can ultimately cause a delay in the fulfillment of God's plan for us. *Learning To Soar* takes you to the root cause of these dilemmas, showing you the '*success-proof*' tactics for rising above your adversary *and* to keep soaring.

With a unique blend of biblical knowledge and spiritual insight, this book brings to light the strategies the enemy uses to launch his attacks. Discover what you need to know to stand strong against the enemy and put him under your feet. The insights found in this book, if practiced, will help you to alter your present situation, as well as prepare and position you for a glorious future.